Designed and published by the Wales Tourist Board,
Brunel House, 2 Fitzalan Road, Cardiff CF2 1UY.
Written by Roger Thomas Freelance Services.
Printed by Mid Wales Litho Ltd.
Typesetting by Evans & Jones Designs.
Copyright © 1996 Wales Tourist Board.
ISBN 1 85013 072 8

Llynnau Mymbyr, Snowdonia

Llyn Brianne in the hills above Llandovery

Accommodation Plus ...

This is more than an accommodation guide. It's a complete holiday planner, with information on Wales's countryside and coastline, its national parks and 'Areas of Outstanding Natural Beauty', its countless castles, craft workshops and attractions.

The great outdoors

Wales's fresh, green surroundings are an increasingly prized asset. It's a pleasant surprise to discover, in this day and age, that you can drive uninterrupted all the way from South to North Wales through a landscape of hills and mountains. Or that you can walk for almost 200 miles along a coast path in Pembrokeshire with only the seabirds for company.

There are no less than three national parks here – the Brecon Beacons, Pembrokeshire Coast and Snowdonia. There are even more official 'Areas of Outstanding Beauty' – the Clwydian Range, Gower Peninsula, Isle of Anglesey, Llŷn Peninsula and Wye Valley. And 40 per cent of Wales's 750-mile seashore has been designated as untouched Heritage Coast.

Attractions and activities

This great natural beauty is a backcloth for all kinds of things to see and do. Wales's rich history is reflected in atmospheric medieval castles and walled towns. Its vibrant artistic and cultural life is expressed at folk festivals and craft workshops.

The country is a stimulating mix of traditional and innovative – old slate caverns have been revitalised as tourist attractions, there are narrow-gauge railways and a unique 'village of the future' dedicated to conservation. And on the activities front, Wales offers everything from walking to watersports, pony trekking to mountain biking.

Wales's varie crafts scene encompasse: everything frc slatecarvers rocking horse makers

2

The Italianate village of Portmeirion

Cader Idris, the mountain above Dolgellau

Green Wales

Point to any part of Wales on the map and you're likely to locate beautiful surroundings – rugged Snowdonia in the north, perhaps, or the high, wild country of the Cambrian Mountains in Mid Wales, or the grassy slopes of the Brecon Beacons in the south.

Wales is green from top to bottom. The quality of its environment is something special – and it intends to keep it this way. There's a wealth of precious, protected places in Wales's many national parks and nature reserves, 'Areas of Outstanding Natural Beauty' and country parks.

Snowdonia and the Brecon Beacons

These two national parks are very different in character. Snowdonia is a dramatic jumble of rocky outcrops, tumbling rivers, brooding moors and deep, wooded valleys. The Brecon Beacons, in contrast, are smooth, grassy and open, offering a rare sense of space and freedom.

The Snowdonia National Park takes its name from Snowdon, the highest mountain in England and Wales. It's a huge area of 845 square miles, extending southwards all the way to Machynlleth. The 519-square-mile Brecon Beacons National Park also covers a lot of ground, from the Wales/England border almost as far as Swansea.

Wild Wales, verdant vales

Wales's undisturbed rural heartlands lie in Mid Wales, an area of rolling border country, lakes and mountains. When people speak of 'Wild Wales' they refer to the remote wildernesses of Plynlimon and the Cambrian Mountains, or the silent hills and marshlands around Tregaron where the rare red kite has made its home, or the spectacular old drover's road that climbs across the 'roof of Wales' to Abergwesyn.

Wales also has its pastoral, sheltered side along valleys such as the lovely vales of Conwy and Clwyd in the north, and the Teifi and Towy in the south.

Areas of outstanding beauty

Possibly the loveliest valley of them all is the Wye Valley, an 'Area of Outstanding Natural Beauty' which runs northwards from Chepstow to Monmouth through thickly wooded hillsides. And in North Wales there's another AONB – the Clwydian Range, an exhilarating line of rounded hills standing guard over green border country and the rich farmlands of the Vale of Clwyd.

Brecon Beacons National Park

Coasting Along

Wales's 750-mile coastline has something for everyone – lively resorts and secluded coves, salty old fishing villages and modern marinas, popular beaches and remote bays.

Worms Head, Gower Peninsula

Beside the seaside

For entertainment-packed seaside holidays, there's the sandy North Wales coast with its string of attractive resorts – elegant Llandudno (where you'll find Wales's best selection of hotels and guest houses) and the colourful, happy-go-lucky appeal of Colwyn Bay, Rhyl and Prestatyn.

Along the Mid Wales coast, Aberystwyth is an attractive mix of Victorian and modern influences. Barmouth and Tywyn, with their fine beaches and mountain-backed settings, are also popular spots, while picturesque Aberdovey attracts sailors as well as holidaymakers.

South Wales's long coastline offers everything from all the fun of the fair at Barry Island and Porthcawl to stylish Saundersfoot and Georgian Tenby.

Away from it all

Wales's national parklands, 'Areas of Outstanding Natural Beauty' and Heritage Coast are made for the quieter style of seaside holiday. The Isle of Anglesey, fringed with vast dunes, rocky promontories and beaches, is dotted with charming little resorts like Rhosneigr, Beaumaris and Benllech.

Anglesey and the Llŷn Peninsula are official AONBs. Along Llŷn's spectacular shores you'll discover more splendid, secluded beaches, towering cliff scenery, and pretty places to stay such as Abersoch, Criccieth and Nefyn.

There's a grand sweep of coastline, from north to south, along Cardigan Bay. Here, you can get lost amongst the dunes of Shell Island near Harlech, or explore the coves and grassy headlands of Ceredigion's Heritage Coast (don't miss Mwnt, a little jewel, or the quaysides at New Quay and Aberaeron).

Pembrokeshire is another – and bigger – jewel. The Pembrokeshire Coast National Park is one of Europe's finest stretches of coastal natural beauty. Wherever you choose – Newport, Fishguard or St David's in the north, Newgale, Broad Haven or Dale in the west, Tenby or Saundersfoot in the south – you'll be amongst breathtaking coastal scenery.

There's more great beauty along the endless sands of Carmarthen Bay where Dylan Thomas sought his inspiration, and the magnificent Gower Peninsula. Gower's sheltered sandy bays and sea-cliffs enjoy a special status – the peninsula was the first part of Britain to be declared an 'Area of Outstanding Natural Beauty'.

Porthdinllaen on the Llŷn Peninsula

An Eventful Year

Wales is an eventful place, with an wide-ranging programme of festivals and fairs, artistic and sporting gatherings running throughout the year. Wales's most traditional cultural festival is the *eisteddfod* (which means 'sitting together'). You can also listen to world-class jazz at Brecon and Llangollen, mix with international literary stars at Hay-on-Wye, enjoy a colourful countryside jamboree at Builth Wells, or take a trip back to Victorian times at Llandrindod Wells.

Here, we've listed just some of the events on offer, beginning with the main activities. More details are contained in the Wales Arts Season '96 brochure and general Events Wales list. Both are available free from Wales Tourist Board, Davis Street, Cardiff CF1 2FU.

End of May-end of December
Mid Wales Festival of the Countryside

A festival which brings together over 500 events taking place throughout beautiful Mid Wales – bird-watching, guided walks, arts and crafts, sheepdog trials, farm and garden visits. David Bellamy, a keen supporter, has called it 'the role model for sustainable tourism'. Tel (01686) 625384

24 May-2 June
Hay Festival of Literature

Hay-on-Wye, the borderland 'town of books', provides an ideal setting for this literary festival with an international reputation. Attracts leading writers, poets and celebrities. Tel (01497) 821217

9-14 July
Llangollen International Musical Eisteddfod

A colourful, cosmopolitan gathering of singers and dancers from all over the world perform in the beautiful little town of Llangollen. A unique festival first held in

1947 to help heal the wounds of war by bringing the peoples of the world together – 1996 is its 50th anniversary. Tel (01978) 860236

22-25 July
Royal Welsh Agricultural Show

Four days of fascination – and a show that attracts a wide audience to Builth Wells, not just from the farming community but from all walks of life. One of Wales's premier events, held in the heart of the country, covering all aspects of agriculture – and a lot more besides. Tel (01982) 553683

3-10 August
Royal National Eisteddfod

Wales's most important cultural gathering, dating back to 1176, and held at a different venue each year. A festival dedicated to Welsh, Britain's oldest living language, with competitions, choirs, concerts, stands and exhibitions. Translation facilities available. This year's event will be held at Llandeilo. Tel (01222) 763777

9-11 August
Brecon Jazz

The streets of Brecon come alive with the sounds of summer jazz. A great three-day international festival with a wonderful atmosphere, which attracts the top names from the world of jazz. Over 80 concerts by bands and solo artists held throughout the town, both indoors and in the open air. Tel (01874) 625557

17-25 August
Llandrindod Wells Victorian Festival

The Mid Wales spa town of Llandrindod Wells celebrates its Victorian past. The festival includes street theatre, walks, talks, drama, exhibitions and music – all with a Victorian flavour. Tel (01597) 823441

Events for Everyone

February
17
Wales v Scotland International Rugby Union, Cardiff Arms Park
26
Llandudno Beer Festival

March
1
St David's Day Concert, St David's Hall, Cardiff
8-10
Folk Weekend, Llanwrtyd Wells
16
Wales v France International Rugby Union, Cardiff Arms Park
26
Conwy Seed Fair

April
14
Welsh Festival of Dressage, Usk Showground
26-5 May
Holyhead Arts Festival

May
1-31
Wrexham Maelor Arts Festival, Wrexham
2-6
Women's Welsh Open, St Pierre Golf Club, nr Chepstow
3-6
Landsker Walking Festival, Narberth
4
Dee and Clwyd Festival of Music Choral Concert, Corwen
9-12
Euro Wales 96 (Inter-European Emergency Medical and Rescue Services Exhibition), Merthyr Tydfil
Llantilio Crossenny Festival
10-12
Llangollen International Jazz Festival

17-19
Mid Wales May Festival, Newtown
18
Man versus Horse Marathon, Llanwrtyd Wells
Ruthin Twinning Festival
25-1 June
St David's Cathedral Festival
25-2 June
Gŵyl Beaumaris Festival (also Craft Fair 25-28 May)
26-27
City of Swansea Show
27-1 June
International Animation Festival, Cardiff
Urdd National Eisteddfod (Youth Eisteddfod), Johnstown, nr Wrexham

June
8
Llangollen Choral Festival
19-23
Criccieth Festival of Music and the Arts
21-23
Gŵyl Ifan - Welsh Folk Dancing Festival, Cardiff and district
22-28
Barmouth to Fort William Three Peaks Yacht Race
22-29
Gregynog Festival, nr Newtown.
29
RAF St Athan At Home Day, St Athan, nr Barry.

July
5-7
Beyond the Border - The Welsh International Festival of Storytelling, St Donat's Castle, nr Llantwit Major
Morris in the Forest Festival (Morris dancing, forest walks, etc), Llanwrtyd Wells

6-13
Gŵyl Werin y Cnapan, Ffostrasol, nr Llandysul
11-20
Welsh Proms '96, St David's Hall, Cardiff
13-14
Mid Wales Festival of Transport, Powis Castle, Welshpool
Wales International Kite Festival, Monmouth
15-27
Gower Music Festival
20-27
Fishguard Music Festival
20-2 Aug
Musicfest - Aberystwyth International Music Festival and Summer School
21-28
Ian Rush International Soccer Tournament (youth soccer), Aberystwyth
29-4 Aug
Gŵyl Conwy Festival

August
4-10
Conwy River Festival
8-9
United Counties Show, Carmarthen
8-11
Mountain Bike Festival, Llanwrtyd Wells
10-11
Caergwrle Historical Festival, nr Wrexham
17-24
West Wales Celtic Watersports Festival, Milford Haven and Waterway
20-28 (provisional)
Vale of Glamorgan Festival, Vale of Glamorgan and Cardiff

24-31
Presteigne Festival of Music and the Arts
26
World Bog-Snorkelling Championships, Llanwrtyd Wells

September
6-13
Barmouth Arts Festival
13
Conwy Honey Fair
15-21
North Wales Music Festival, St Asaph
17-20
Welsh International Four Days of Walks, Llanwrtyd Wells
20-28
Tenby Arts Festival

October
1-31
Swansea Festival
12-20
Llandudno October Festival
17-20
Welsh International Four Day Cycle Ride, Llanwrtyd Wells
24-26
Abertawe Festival for Young Musicians, University College, Swansea

November
9-17
Welsh International Film Festival, Aberystwyth
15-24
Mid Wales Beer Festival, Llanwrtyd Wells

December
3
Royal Welsh Agricultural Winter Fair, Builth Wells

History and Heritage

Wales's past is etched in its landscape. In your travels, you'll come across prehistoric and Roman remains, mighty medieval castles, manor houses and mansions, and a fascinating industrial heritage.

Caerphilly Castle

Ancient stones and medieval strongholds

Skeletal Pentre Ifan Cromlech in Pembrokeshire's Preseli Hills is one of many prehistoric monuments scattered throughout Wales. Thousands of years later, the Romans left camps, roadways, an extraordinary amphitheatre and bath-house at Caerleon and unique gold mine at Pumsaint. But more than anything else, Wales is famous for its castles – mighty medieval monuments such as Caernarfon, Conwy and Caerphilly, as well as dramatic ruins like Carreg Cennen, Llandeilo and remote Castell-y-Bere hidden beneath Cader Idris.

Historic houses

History also lives on at Llancaiach Fawr, a restored Tudor manor house in the Rhymney Valley which recreates the times of the Civil War. You can glimpse into grand country houses at National Trust properties such as Plas Newydd on Anglesey, Welshpool's Powis Castle and Erddig near Wrexham (an unusual 'upstairs, downstairs' house). Dignified Tredegar House at Newport is another mansion with two sides to its personality – a glittering interior together with preserved servants' quarters.

Industrial memories

In Wales, you'll discover gripping monuments to the era of coal, slate, iron and steel. 'King Coal's' reign is remembered at places like the Big Pit Mining Museum, Blaenafon, and the Rhondda Heritage Park. North Wales's slate industry has a successful modern spin-off at the popular Llechwedd Slate Caverns, Blaenau Ffestiniog – and slate is again the theme at the Gloddfa Ganol Mine, also in Blaenau Ffestiniog, and Llanberis's Welsh Slate Museum.

At Your Service

Welcome Host

Service and hospitality are as important as good accommodation and good food. We attach top priority to customer care – which is what our 'Welcome Host' scheme is all about. Open to everyone from taxi drivers to hotel staff, the scheme places the empha. on friendliness and first-class service.

Welcome Host is part of a fine tradition in Wales – a tradition embodied in the welcoming greeting of *croeso*. Look out for the Welcome Host certificate or badge – it's a sure sign of the best in Welsh hospitality and service.

A Taste of Wales

Good food is another important ingredient of any holiday. In Wales, you're in for a treat, for there's been an explosion of talent

on the cooking scene. Throughout the country – in restaurants and hotels, inns and bistros – talented chefs are preparing everything from traditional favourites such as *cawl* (a nourishing, hearty broth) to modern, imaginative dishes, often cooked with a lighter touch.

A sign of good taste

When you travel through Wales you'll see many establishments displaying the Taste of Wales-*Blas ar Gymru* plaque. The scheme was created to encourage and promote a distinctive culinary identity through the use of local ingredients as well as traditional and innovative Welsh recipes. Wales is fortunate to have such an abundant larder of fresh, local produce, including superb seafoods, top-quality Welsh lamb, and wonderful cheeses. Taste of Wales members must use Welsh ingredients, cook them in a competent and creative manner and offer Welsh hospitality with enthusiasm. And quality is being further encouraged through a grading scheme which will be introduced during 1996.

So Accessible

One of Wales's big advantages is its ease of access. It's only a few hours by road and rail from most of the UK's main centres. Travel to Wales doesn't take up much time or money, so you can enjoy your holiday or short break to the full. And when you arrive, you'll be back in the days when driving was a pleasure on traffic-free highways and byways.

By car

Travel to South and West Wales is easy on the M4 and onward dual carriageway systems. The A55 North

Wales coast 'Expressway' whisks traffic past the old bottlenecks, including Conwy. Mid Wales is easily reached by the M54 which links with the M6/M5/M1.

Driving around Wales is a delight, for most highways remain blissfully quiet and uncrowded apart from a few peak summer weekends.

By rail

Fast and frequent Great Western InterCity services run between London Paddington and Cardiff (via Reading and Swindon), taking only 2 hours. This hourly service (every half hour at peak times) also runs to Newport, Bridgend, Port Talbot, Neath and Swansea, with onward connections to West Wales. Fast InterCity trains also link London (Euston) with the North Wales coast, serving both Bangor and Holyhead, and Newcastle/York to South Wales.

In addition, Regional Railways operates a direct service from London Waterloo (via Woking and Basingstoke) to Cardiff and other main stations in South and West Wales. Regional Railways also runs other services into Wales. There are convenient and comfortable 'Alphaline' trains to Cardiff (and other destinations in South and West Wales) from:

Manchester/the North West;
Brighton/Portsmouth/Salisbury/Southampton;
The West of England/Bristol;
Birmingham/Gloucester.
'Alphaline' also operates from Birmingham to Aberystwyth and other Mid Wales resorts via Shrewsbury.

A 'North West Express' service operates from Manchester to the North Wales coast and Holyhead via Crewe and Chester.

Exploring Wales by train is a delight. Scenic routes include the beautiful Heart of Wales line from Shrewsbury to Swansea, the Conwy Valley line from Llandudno Junction to Blaenau Ffestiniog, and the Cambrian Coast line, which runs along the mountain-backed shoreline from Pwllheli to Machynlleth and Aberystwyth.

Ask about the money-saving unlimited-travel Rover and Ranger fares, some of which include the use of bus services.

By coach

National Express provides a nationwide network of express coach services. Convenient services to Wales operate from London's Victoria Coach Station and from almost all other major towns and cities in England and Scotland.

Towns and resorts throughout Wales are, of course, connected by a whole range of local and regional services. Details from Tourist Information Centres and local bus stations. You can travel cross-country by the TrawsCambria service running between Cardiff and Bangor (via Aberystwyth). Within North and Mid Wales you can combine coach and rail services through unlimited-travel Rover and Ranger tickets (see 'By rail' for details).

Further information

Please see 'Further Information' at the back of this guide for rail and coach travel information offices, plus details of sea and air services to Wales.

MILEAGE CHART

	MILES	JOURNEY TIME BY CAR
Birmingham – Aberystwyth	125	2 hrs 49 mins
Canterbury – Cardiff	219	3 hrs 56 mins
Coventry – Barmouth	133	2 hrs 51 mins
Exeter – Swansea	161	2 hrs 25 mins
Leeds – Llandudno	131	2 hrs 3 mins
London – Cardiff	155	2 hrs 40 mins
London – Tenby	245	4 hrs 7 mins
Manchester – Caernarfon	110	1 hr 58 mins
Nottingham – Swansea	202	3 hrs 10 mins
Peterborough – Aberystwyth	208	4 hrs 30 mins
Newcastle-upon-Tyne – Llandudno	230	3 hrs 56 mins
Reading – Carmarthen	177	2 hrs 40 mins
York – Welshpool	155	2 hrs 55 mins

Where to Stay

The remainder of this guide is filled with a great choice of places to stay. It's not surprising that bed and breakfasting in Wales is so popular. It's friendly. It's flexible. And it's great value for money. You'll not pay more that £20 per person per night for any B&B featured in this guide – and in most cases, the price is considerably less.

You can make your choice in confidence, because the accommodation has been thoroughly checked out by a visit from one of our approved inspectors. Not only that, but we also clearly spell out the quality and standards for you.

Making the grade

Look out first for the GRADES – they're your guide to QUALITY. In determining them, the inspectors take into account standards of comfort, service, food, atmosphere and so on.

APPROVED	- Good
COMMENDED	- Very Good
HIGHLY COMMENDED	- Excellent
DE LUXE	- A special accolade representing exceptional comfort and service

Focus on facilities

CROWNS tell you how WELL EQUIPPED the accommodation is. The more facilities, the higher the Crown rating. The range runs from Listed (clean and comfortable accommodation) to Five Crowns (an extensive range of facilities and services).

Award-winners

If you want extra-special guest house or farmhouse accommodation, look out for the places which have won the coveted Wales Tourist Board Award (all Award-winners will have the Highly Commended or De Luxe grade). Award-winning establishments are supremely comfortable – they're as good as many a hotel.

Accommodating wheelchair users

 Accessible to a wheelchair user travelling independently

 Accessible to a wheelchair user travelling with assistance

 Accessible to a wheelchair user able to walk a few paces and up a maximum of three steps

For further details, please see 'Information for visitors with disabilities' in the 'Further Information/Useful Addresses' section of this guide.

PLEASE NOTE

All gradings and classifications were correct at the time of going to press. Inspections are on-going and improvements made by establishments may have resulted in a revised grade or classification since publication. Please check when booking. Further information on the grading and Crown schemes is available from the Visitor Services Unit, Wales Tourist Board, Davis Street, Cardiff CF1 2FU.

Tenby on the Pembrokeshire coast

Making Your Booking

Book direct

Telephone or write to the place of your choice direct. It's as simple as that. If you phone, please check the prices and follow up the call with a letter of confirmation enclosing whatever deposit you've agreed with the proprietor.

Prices

There's nothing more expensive in this guide than a per person price of £20 a night. You'll find that most rates quoted are even less.

Single rates are for ONE PERSON in a single room. Double rates are for TWO PEOPLE sharing a double or twin room. There may be supplements for private bath/shower and single occupancy of a double/twin room.

All prices quoted include VAT at the current rate (17$\frac{1}{2}$%). Prices and other specific holiday information in this guide were supplied to the Wales Tourist Board during June–September 1995. So do check all prices and facilities before confirming your booking.

Book through a TIC

Look out for this symbol on the following pages. It means that you can book the featured accommodation through any networked Tourist Information Centre. Please see the TIC list at the back of this guide for more details on this Bed Booking Service.

Children stay free

Many hotels, guest houses and farmhouses offer free accommodation for children if sharing their parents' room (you only pay for their meals). It's always worth asking about reductions, for most operators will offer child discounts. Family holiday hotels, especially in major resorts, also cater for one-parent families.

Deposits

Most operators will ask for a deposit when a reservation is being made. Some establishments may request payment in advance of arrival.

Cancellation and insurance

When you confirm a holiday booking, please bear in mind that you are entering a legally binding contract which entitles the proprietor to compensation if you fail to take up the accommodation. It's always wise to arrange holiday insurance to cover you for cancellation and other unforeseen eventualities. If you have to alter your travel plans, please advise the holiday operator or proprietor immediately.

Looking after your best interests

We care about our visitors' views and encourage you to make any comments you may have about your stay to the proprietor of the establishment at the time of your visit. In this way it may be possible to make your stay even more pleasurable and to arrange for new facilities and services to be provided in the future. If you need to get in touch with the Wales Tourist Board about any aspect of your stay please write to the Visitor Services Unit, Wales Tourist Board, Davis Street, Cardiff CF1 2FU. We will let you have a reply to your letter within 15 working days of its receipt.

Key to Symbols

H	Hotel
GH	Guest House
FH	Farmhouse
	Total number of bedrooms
	Number of en-suite bedrooms
	Recipient of the Wales Tourist Board Guest House and Farmhouse Award
	Welcome Host (minimum of 50% of staff trained)
P	Private car parking/garage facilities at establishment
	Dogs/pets accepted into establishment by arrangement
C	Children under 12 accommodated free if sharing parents' room (meals charged extra)
	Liquor licence
	Central heating throughout
	Areas provided for non-smokers
	Totally non-smoking establishment
	Evening meals available by prior arrangement
i	Accommodation may be booked through Networked Tourist Information Centres
	Railway Station

Please note: The symbols, together with the descriptive wording in the following accommodation advertisements, have been provided by the proprietors.

Using This Guide

Please note that the borders between each area are only approximate. Places on or close to the border may choose to be listed under the area or areas of their choice.

It's easy to find your way around this guide. The rest of the book is filled with 'where to stay' information presented as follows. Firstly, we divide the accommodation up into Wales's 12 holiday areas (see the map and index opposite). Then within each individual area, the resorts, towns and villages are listed alphabetically. Each place has a map reference enabling you to pinpoint it on the detailed gridded maps at the back of the book.

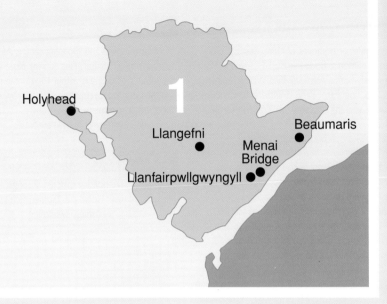

Holyhead

Llangefni

Beaumaris

Menai
Bridge

Llanfairpwllgwyngyll

This island is a place of great natural beauty, history and heritage. The coastline is astonishingly varied – from the dunes of Newborough to the sea-cliffs of Holyhead Mountain and the open sands of Red Wharf Bay. Anglesey, with its small, stylish resorts, is the perfect destination for the quieter seaside holiday.

If you can drag yourself away from the beach you'll find a huge range of places to visit – ancient burial chambers, the mansion of Plas Newydd, Beaumaris Castle and the award-winning Anglesey Sea Zoo to name but a few. If you're a birdwatcher, bring your binoculars to the cliffs at South Stack or the sands at Malltraeth. For sailors, there are the sheltered waters of the Menai Strait between Anglesey and the mainland of North Wales.

It's a fact…

Thomas Telford's elegant Menai Suspension Bridge connecting Anglesey to mainland Wales was opened in 1826. The nearby Britannia Bridge, which carries road and rail traffic, dates from 1850. Most of the island's 125-mile coastline has been declared an 'Area of Outstanding Natural Beauty' (designated in 1966). The world-famous town with the longest name is Llanfairpwllgwyngyllgogerychwyrndrobwllllantysiliogogogoch, which means 'St Mary's (Church) by the white aspen over the whirlpool, and St Tysilio's (Church) by the red cave'. Locals make do with Llanfairpwll.

Ad4 Brynsiencyn

Anglesey hamlet near shores of Menai Strait, looking across to Snowdonia. Bodowyr Burial Chamber, Plas Newydd stately home, Anglesey Bird World, Anglesey Model Village, Foel Farm Park, Bryntirion Open Farm, and award-winning Anglesey Sea Zoo all nearby.

Aa2 Holyhead ⇌

Stands on Holy Island, linked by causeway to Anglesey. Port for Irish ferries. Roman remains and maritime museum in town. Sailing school. Sea angling, cliff and hill walking. Enjoy the sight of seabirds, coastal flora and the view from the cliffs to South Stack Lighthouse. RSPB centre located on cliffs. Penrhos Coastal Park on approach to the town.

Ac2 Llanerchymedd

Central Anglesey village with easy access to island's beaches. Visit Din Llugwy, prehistoric remains of fortified village, the working windmill at Llanddeusant and the Llyn Alaw Visitor Centre.

Ad3 Llanfairpwllgwyngyll ⇌

Famous for its 58-letter name of Llanfairpwllgwyngyllgogerychwyrndrobwllllantysilio-gogogoch which means 'St Mary's church by the white aspen near the violent whirlpool and St Tysilio's church by the red cave'. Fine crafts centre with extensive choice of products. Plas Newydd stately home nearby. Marvellous views from the 27m/90ft Marquess of Anglesey Column. Bryn Celli Ddu Burial Chamber.

Ac4 Llangaffo

On an Anglesey crossroads in the south-western corner of the island. Good birdwatching along Malltraeth Sands and Marsh, excellent, spacious beach at Newborough (drive through the forest), award-winning Anglesey Sea Zoo at Brynsiencyn.

Ad3 Llangefni

Market town and shopping centre, Anglesey's administrative 'capital'. Fine touring base; almost all of the island's coastline is within 10–15 mile radius. Many attractions and prehistoric sites nearby. Art gallery with historic displays, sports centre. Trout fishing in nearby Cefni reservoir.

Aa3 Trearddur Bay

Most attractive holiday spot set amongst low cliffs on Holy Island near Holyhead. Golden sands, golf, sailing, fishing, swimming.

South Stack, Isle of Anglesey

Brynsiencyn Holyhead Llanerchymedd Llanfairpwllgwyngyll Llangaffo

---

GH | Fron Guest House

Brynsiencyn,
Isle of Anglesey
LL61 6TX
Tel: (01248) 430310

HIGHLY COMMENDED

Comfortable traditional B&B in centrally heated farmhouse. Peaceful off road situation with magnificent views. Ideal location for Anglesey and Snowdonia. Many tourist attractions, beaches, golf and fishing nearby. Tea/coffee. TV's in all rooms. Sunlounge, patio with outdoor heated swimming pool in summer. Several pubs and restaurants nearby for evening meals. **i**

		SINGLE PER PERSON B&B		DOUBLE FOR 2 PERSONS B&B			3
							1
		MIN £	MAX £	MIN £	MAX £	OPEN	
		15.00	-	29.00	32.00	3-11	

GH | Roselea

26 Holborn Road,
Holyhead,
Isle of Anglesey
LL65 2AT
Tel: (01407) 764391

COMMENDED

Homely guest house, five minutes from ferry, station, beaches and golf course. Ideally situated for fishing, bird watching, climbing and walking. Hot and cold water, tea/coffee and TV all bedrooms. TV lounge. Catering for early and late ferry travellers, packed lunches available. Rooms furnished to a high standard. Prop. Mrs S Foxley.

		SINGLE PER PERSON B&B		DOUBLE FOR 2 PERSONS B&B			3
							-
		MIN £	MAX £	MIN £	MAX £	OPEN	
		16.00	16.00	24.00	30.00	1-12	

FH | Drws y Coed

Drws y Coed,
Llanerchymedd,
Isle of Anglesey
LL71 8AD
Tel: (01248) 470473

AWARD HIGHLY COMMENDED

With wonderful panoramic views of Snowdonia, this beautifully appointed farmhouse on a 550 acre working farm is situated in peaceful, wooded countryside in the centre of Anglesey. Beautifully decorated en-suite bedrooms with TV, clock-radio, hairdryer, tea tray. Central heating. Log fire and games room. Lovely private walks. Visitors return year after year. Farm Holiday Guide diploma award. **i**

		SINGLE PER PERSON B&B		DOUBLE FOR 2 PERSONS B&B			3
							3
		MIN £	MAX £	MIN £	MAX £	OPEN	
		-	20.00	36.00	40.00	1-12	

FH | Tyddyn Goblet

Brynsiencyn,
Isle of Anglesey
LL61 6TZ
Tel: (01248) 430296

AWARD HIGHLY COMMENDED

Character farmhouse set back 200 yards from A4080 Newborough road. Private suite consists of two ground floor bedrooms with colour television and tea making facilities. Evening dinner optional. Attractive lounge and pleasant dining room with separate tables. 5 miles from Britannia Bridge, convenient for Snowdonia and the North Wales coast. Many main Anglesey attractions nearby. **i**

		SINGLE PER PERSON B&B		DOUBLE FOR 2 PERSONS B&B			2
							2
		MIN £	MAX £	MIN £	MAX £	OPEN	
		15.00	16.00	28.00	32.00	1-11	

GH | Tan-y-Cytiau Country Guest House

South Stack Road,
Holyhead,
Isle of Anglesey
LL65 1YH
Tel: (01407) 762763

HIGHLY COMMENDED

Country house peacefully situated in 3 acres of lovely gardens on slopes of Holyhead Mountain with magnificent views from all rooms. Ideal for walking and bird watching, adjacent to RSPB reserve. Good sailing facilities in large sheltered harbour. Excellent 18 hole golf course nearby. Convenient for ferry to Ireland. Write or telephone for brochure. **i**

		SINGLE PER PERSON B&B		DOUBLE FOR 2 PERSONS B&B			7
							-
		MIN £	MAX £	MIN £	MAX £	OPEN	
		18.50	20.00	37.00	37.00	3-9	

GH | Carreg Goch

Llanedwen,
Llanfairpwllgwyngyll,
Isle of Anglesey LL61 6EZ
Tel: (01248) 430315

Adjacent N.T. property of Plas Newydd, stands back from A4080 and is surrounded by 4 acres of gardens. 2 ground floor bedrooms have tea making facilities, hot and cold and separate toilet. Both have central heating, share a private patio and have glorious views of Snowdonia. There is a guest bath/shower room and a TV lounge. Convenient to beaches and mountains. Brochure Mrs Kirkland. **i**

		SINGLE PER PERSON B&B		DOUBLE FOR 2 PERSONS B&B			2
							-
		MIN £	MAX £	MIN £	MAX £	OPEN	
		18.00	-	30.00	30.00	3-10	

GH | Bryn Awel

Edmund Street,
Holyhead,
Isle of Anglesey LL65 1SA
Tel: (01407) 762948

L

Friendly comfortable family run guest house, centrally situated, five minutes car ferry, five minutes shops. TV lounge. Hot and cold water, tea making facilities in all rooms. Sandy beach, golf course, one mile. Day trips Ireland. Good home cooking, pleasant family atmosphere. Hospitality guaranteed, children welcome. All ferries to and from Ireland catered for. **i**

		SINGLE PER PERSON B&B		DOUBLE FOR 2 PERSONS B&B			3
							-
		MIN £	MAX £	MIN £	MAX £	OPEN	
		13.00	15.00	25.00	30.00	1-12	

GH | Wavecrest

93 Newry Street,
Holyhead,
Isle of Anglesey
LL65 1HU
Tel: (01407) 763637

COMMENDED

Situated in a quiet location, yet only two minutes from ferry teminal, town centre and yards from sea. Ideal to break journey en-route to/from Ireland. Late arrivals, early departures welcome. All rooms furnished to high standard with beverage facilities, colour satellite TV, radio alarms. Large family en-suites available. AA Recommended, friendly welcome awaits. **i**

		SINGLE PER PERSON B&B		DOUBLE FOR 2 PERSONS B&B			4
							2
		MIN £	MAX £	MIN £	MAX £	OPEN	
		15.00	20.00	26.00	32.00	1-12	

FH | Plas Llangaffo Farmhouse

Llangaffo,
Isle of Anglesey
LL60 6LR
Tel: (01248) 440452

L

Peaceful location, with large garden, ideally suited for pets and children. Close to Newborough Forest and Llandwyn Bay. Horse riding available in our full size, all weather menagé. Free range eggs and home-made marmalade for breakfast. Vegetarians catered for. An ideal base to visit Ireland. Phone Ann or David for brochure. **i**

		SINGLE PER PERSON B&B		DOUBLE FOR 2 PERSONS B&B			5
							-
		MIN £	MAX £	MIN £	MAX £	OPEN	
		14.00	14.00	28.00	28.00	1-12	

Llangefni Trearddur Bay

GH	Argraig

HIGHLY COMMENDED

Llangristiolus,
Bodorgan,
Isle of Anglesey
LL62 5PW
Tel: (01248) 724390

Homely B&B with twin/double room, with H/C, central heating, private bathroom, tea/coffee facility, colour TV. Children welcome. Off road parking. Located 0.5 miles west of A5 road on the B4422, first house on left after village sign of Llangristiolus. Tariff from £16.00 per person per night. A warm Welsh welcome awaits you. *i*

P ⊞ ✕	SINGLE PER PERSON B&B		DOUBLE FOR 2 PERSONS B&B		🛏 1 🛏 1
	MIN £ 16.00	MAX £ 17.00	MIN £ 32.00	MAX £ 34.00	OPEN 3-10

GH	Moranedd Guest House

Trearddur Road,
Trearddur Bay,
Isle of Anglesey LL65 2UE
Tel: (01407) 860324

Moranedd is a lovely guest house with a sun patio overlooking 0.75 acre garden. Only 5 minutes' stroll to the beach, shops, restaurants, sailing and golf clubs. The bedrooms are large, well-furnished with wash basins and tea making facilities. Residents' lounge with colour TV. AA and RAC Listed. *i*

P ⊞	SINGLE PER PERSON B&B		DOUBLE FOR 2 PERSONS B&B		🛏 6 🛏 -
	MIN £ 14.00	MAX £ 14.00	MIN £ 28.00	MAX £ 28.00	OPEN 1-12

Journey Through Wales
• Magnificently produced book, the ideal gift or memento
• High quality photographs with accompanying text take you on a tour of Wales
• Classic views of Wales's scenic mountains and coastline
• A complete pictorial record – everything from powerful castles to colourful craft workshops, picturesque villages to narrow-gauge railways
£4.80 inc. p&p
(see 'Get Yourself a Guide' at the end of the book)

Trearddur Bay

22

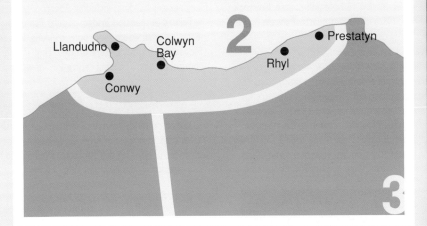

Llandudno •   Colwyn Bay •   2   • Prestatyn

Rhyl •

Conwy

North Wales's sandy coastal strip is famous for its popular mixture of big beaches, colourful attractions and family entertainment. But within this formula there's scope for variety. Historic Conwy, with its ancient walls and castle, still retains a medieval air. Llandudno, the stately 'Queen' of the Welsh resorts, remains faithful to its Victorian roots while at the same time catering for the needs of today's visitors. For sheer seaside harmony, there's nothing quite like the view along its seafront from the headland above. Colwyn Bay, Rhyl and Prestatyn offer unpretentious fun and amusement, with huge beaches and an even larger choice of attractions, including the marvellous Welsh Mountain Zoo (Colwyn Bay), the Sun Centre (Rhyl) and the Nova Centre (Prestatyn).

It's a fact…

Llandudno's pier is over 900m/3000ft long. The resort's alpine-style Cabin Lift, one of the longest in Britain, carries passengers by cablecar for over a mile from the seafront to the summit of the Great Orme headland. Conwy has Britain's 'smallest house', a tiny fisherman's cottage on the quay. The Welsh Mountain Zoo at Colwyn Bay is owned by the Zoological Society of Wales, an educational and scientific charity. Rhyl's 73m-/240ft-high Skytower offers spectacular views from Snowdonia to Liverpool. Prestatyn is at one end of the 168-mile Offa's Dyke Path.

Bd4 Abergele

Convenient centre, located between Colwyn Bay and Rhyl, for exploring the popular coastal resorts. Wooded walks nearby, 18-hole golf course, livestock market. Miles of sand at nearby Pensarn.

Bc4 Colwyn Bay

Bustling seaside resort with large sandy beach. Promenade amusements. Good touring centre for Snowdonia. Leisure centre, Eirias Park, Dinosaur World, famous Mountain Zoo with Chimpanzee World. Puppet theatre. Golf, tennis, riding and other sports. Quieter Rhos on Sea at western end of bay.

Bb4 Conwy

Historic town with mighty castle and complete ring of medieval town walls. Dramatic estuary setting. Many ancient buildings including Aberconwy House. Telford Suspension Bridge, popular fish quay, spectacular wall walks. Golf, pony trekking, Butterfly House, aquarium, pleasure cruises. Tiny 'smallest house' on quay. Touring centre for Snowdonia.

Bd3 Kinmel Bay

Located on sandy stretch of the popular North Wales coast just west of Rhyl. Good beach, host of seaside attractions on the doorstep. Well placed for exploring the beautiful Vale of Clwyd.

Bb3 Llandudno

Premier coastal resort of North Wales with everything the holidaymaker needs. Two beaches, spacious promenade, Victorian pier, excellent shopping. Donkey rides. Punch and Judy, ski slope. Alice in Wonderland exhibition, art gallery, museum, old copper mines open to the public, splendid North Wales Theatre. Visit the Great Orme headland above the resort and ride by cabinlift or tramway. Conference centre. Many daily coach excursions.

Be3 Prestatyn

Family seaside resort on popular North Wales coast. Entertainment galore at superb Nova Centre including heated swimming pools and aquashute. Sailing, swimming on long, sandy coastline. Close to pastoral Vale of Clwyd and Clwydian Range.

Bb3 Rhos on Sea

Attractive seaside village linking Llandudno and Colwyn Bay with promenade, beach, golf, water-skiing, puppet theatre. Colwyn Bay Mountain Zoo nearby.

Conwy Castle

Abergele   Colwyn Bay   Conwy   Kinmel Bay   Llandudno

GH   The Haven Guest House

Towyn Road,
Belgrano,
Abergele
LL22 9AB
Tel: (01745) 823534

Cliff and Barbara Pilley welcome you to the Haven, a friendly guest house with single, double and family rooms. Central heating, hot and cold water, shaver points and tea and coffee making facilities (all ingredients supplied). Lounge with colour TV, dining room has separate tables. Access to rooms and lounge at all reasonable times.

	SINGLE PER PERSON B&B		DOUBLE FOR 2 PERSONS B&B		🛏 3 🛁 -
	MIN £	MAX £	MIN £	MAX £	OPEN
	14.00	-	25.00	-	1-12

H   Whitehall Hotel

HIGHLY COMMENDED

51 Cayley Promenade,
Rhos on Sea, Colwyn Bay
LL28 4EP
Tel: (01492) 547296

Small select family run hotel on lovely Cayley Promenade. Ideal location to tour North Wales. Renowned for our excellent cuisine and friendliness. Lovely sea view patio. Sandy beach only yards away. Llandudno, Betws-y-Coed, Conwy, all within easy reach. Car park. Packed lunches available, licensed bar, sea view lounge. A55 expressway very close. AA ★★ RAC Merit Award.

	SINGLE PER PERSON B&B		DOUBLE FOR 2 PERSONS B&B		🛏 13 🛁 9
	MIN £	MAX £	MIN £	MAX £	OPEN
	17.50	20.00	34.00	40.00	4-11

GH   Rosemount Guest House

11 Crugan Avenue,
Kinmel Bay
LL18 5DG
Tel: (01745) 334273

Detached character house set in large garden with ponds and patios. Beamed ceilings, centrally heated. All comfortable bedrooms have vanity sinks, shaver points etc. We have one double on ground floor, one twin and one single. Situated in quiet residential area of small seaside community, 1 mile from resort town of Rhyl. Ideal for touring North Wales and Snowdonia.

	SINGLE PER PERSON B&B		DOUBLE FOR 2 PERSONS B&B		🛏 3 🛁 -
	MIN £	MAX £	MIN £	MAX £	OPEN
	11.95	12.95	23.90	25.90	4-11

H   Lyndale Hotel

410 Abergele Road,
Colwyn Bay
LL29 9AB
Tel: (01492) 515429
Fax: (01492) 518805

This 2 star family hotel offers all bedrooms en-suite, excellent cuisine and friendly service. Car park. Located in the village of Old Colwyn, with views over Colwyn Bay. Ideally central for all beaches, castles and Snowdonia. Inclusive rate for short breaks, group bookings and golf parties available.

	SINGLE PER PERSON B&B		DOUBLE FOR 2 PERSONS B&B		🛏 14 🛁 14
	MIN £	MAX £	MIN £	MAX £	OPEN
	15.00	20.00	30.00	40.00	1-12

GH   Crossroads Guest House

Coed Pella Road,
Colwyn Bay
LL29 7AT
Tel: (01492) 530736

Crossroads is the oldest established guest house in Colwyn Bay, small, homely and tasteful. Central for the wonders of North Wales. Just a short drive to visit the mountains, lakes, fast flowing rivers, forests, with a stunning coastline with castles, stately homes, narrow gauge railways and the underground world of slate mines to explore and be thrilled by in this land of myths and legends. En-suite supplement £3.00 per person.

	SINGLE PER PERSON B&B		DOUBLE FOR 2 PERSONS B&B		🛏 5 🛁 2
	MIN £	MAX £	MIN £	MAX £	OPEN
	12.50	14.00	25.00	28.00	1-12

H   Ashby

HIGHLY COMMENDED

31 Church Walks,
Llandudno
LL30 2HL
Tel: (01492) 875608
Fax: (01492) 875608

Attractive Victorian detached house now a comfortable family run licensed hotel. Located between both shores in quiet tree-lined road close to Great Orme and amenities. Excellent home cooked food, varied menu. Spacious rooms with en-suite facilities, colour TV, beverage makers. All bedrooms no smoking. Centrally heated. A warm welcome awaits you at the Ashby.

	SINGLE PER PERSON B&B		DOUBLE FOR 2 PERSONS B&B		🛏 7 🛁 7
	MIN £	MAX £	MIN £	MAX £	OPEN
	16.50	18.50	33.00	37.00	1-12

H   Marine Hotel

COMMENDED

West Promenade,
Colwyn Bay
LL28 4BP
Tel: (01492) 530295

Superbly situated, AA ★, seafront hotel, close to town centre, pier, theatre and Colwyn Bay B.R. station. All spacious bedrooms with TV, radio and tea making facilities, most have sea view. Family rooms - generous reductions for children. Car parking on premises, non smoking restaurant, licensed.

	SINGLE PER PERSON B&B		DOUBLE FOR 2 PERSONS B&B		🛏 14 🛁 10
	MIN £	MAX £	MIN £	MAX £	OPEN
	15.75	20.00	31.50	40.00	4-10

GH   Pen-y-Bryn

HIGHLY COMMENDED

Lancaster Square,
Conwy
LL32 8DE
Tel: (01492) 596445

Guests are once again invited to sample Pen-y-Bryn's own brand of hospitality and comfort, on offer above their unique 16th century tea rooms. Egon Ronay recommended, all bedrooms have central heating, colour TV, hair dryer, and beverage facilities. Two rooms have en-suite showers and WC. Non smoking throughout. Private car parking available nearby.

	SINGLE PER PERSON B&B		DOUBLE FOR 2 PERSONS B&B		🛏 3 🛁 2
	MIN £	MAX £	MIN £	MAX £	OPEN
	15.00	20.00	30.00	36.00	1-12

Please Note

All the accommodation in this guide has applied for verification/classification and in many instances for grading also. However, at the time of going to press not all establishments had been visited – some of these properties are indicated by the wording 'Awaiting Inspection' or 'Awaiting Grading'.

Llandudno

H Brannock Hotel

36 St David's Road,
Llandudno
LL30 2UH
Tel: (01492) 877483

HIGHLY COMMENDED

Small, homely, family run hotel in quiet, select, level area of town. Convenient for shops, beaches. Ideal base for touring North Wales and Snowdonia. Choice of traditional varied home cooking. Most rooms en suite. Full central heating. Colour TV and tea making facilities in all rooms. Car park. WTB Highly Commended. A friendly welcome awaits you.

	SINGLE PER PERSON B&B		DOUBLE FOR 2 PERSONS B&B			🛏 8
						🛁 5
	MIN £	MAX £	MIN £	MAX £	OPEN	
	15.00	19.00	30.00	38.00	3-11	

H Karden House Hotel

16 Charlton Street,
Llandudno
LL30 2AA
Tel: (01492) 879347/879990

COMMENDED

Conveniently situated for beach, shops and station. Vera and Des Steward provide a friendly, caring service, fresh home cooking, vegetarian/allergy diets catered for. Tea/coffee, central heating, TV, en-suite available, licensed bar, separate lounge. Open Christmas, reductions OAP's - children. Ideally situated for visiting scenic beauty spots, activities on Great Orme; skiing, toboggan run, cable car, tram.

	SINGLE PER PERSON B&B		DOUBLE FOR 2 PERSONS B&B			🛏 10
						🛁 3
	MIN £	MAX £	MIN £	MAX £	OPEN	
	12.00	13.50	24.00	27.00	1-12	

H Tan Lan Hotel

Great Orme's Road,
West Shore,
Llandudno,
LL30 2AR
Tel: (01492) 860221
Fax: (01492) 860221

HIGHLY COMMENDED

Elegant 2 star family hotel offering unique charm and friendly atmosphere. All 18 rooms at ground or first floor level with en-suite facilities and tea makers. Bright airy restaurant serving food of the highest quality and good value. Car park. Ideal position for touring. Easy walk to all local amenities. May we welcome you?

	SINGLE PER PERSON B&B		DOUBLE FOR 2 PERSONS B&B			🛏 18
						🛁 18
	MIN £	MAX £	MIN £	MAX £	OPEN	
	20.00	-	40.00	-	3-10	

H Carmel Private Hotel

17 Craig-y-Don Parade,
Promenade, Llandudno
LL30 1BG
Tel: (01492) 877643

COMMENDED

Situated in a prime position on the main promenade. Carmel welcomes you to a family run hotel with excellent home cooking. Twin ground floor en-suite bedroom, plus all other rooms on two floors, only six en-suite rooms, plus three standard rooms. Colour TV, tea/coffee making facilities in all bedrooms. Conference centre, theatre close by.

	SINGLE PER PERSON B&B		DOUBLE FOR 2 PERSONS B&B			🛏 9
						🛁 6
	MIN £	MAX £	MIN £	MAX £	OPEN	
	14.00	19.00	28.00	33.00	4-10	

H Lynton House Hotel

80 Church Walks,
Llandudno
LL30 2HD
Tel: (01492) 875057/875009

HIGHLY COMMENDED

A small homely hotel fifty yards from the pier. Close to shops, skiing and all amenities. All rooms are decorated to a high standard with en-suite bathroom, colour TV, tea/coffee tray and telephone. Highly recommended home cooking with choice of menu. Vegetarian and special diets catered for. Four poster room available. Car park.

	SINGLE PER PERSON B&B		DOUBLE FOR 2 PERSONS B&B			🛏 12
						🛁 12
	MIN £	MAX £	MIN £	MAX £	OPEN	
	19.50	20.00	39.00	40.00	1-12	

GH Dolwen Guest House

7 St Mary's Road,
Llandudno
LL30 2UB
Tel: (01492) 877757

HIGHLY COMMENDED

Situated within easy reach of shops, beach and new North Wales Theatre. Dolwen is a family run guest house, highly recommended by guests. All bedrooms are en-suite with colour TV, clock radio and tea/coffee making facilities. Home comforts with lounge with colour TV. Special diets catered for. Write/phone for colour brochure. Full fire certificate.

	SINGLE PER PERSON B&B		DOUBLE FOR 2 PERSONS B&B			🛏 3
						🛁 3
	MIN £	MAX £	MIN £	MAX £	OPEN	
	-	-	28.00	30.00	4-10	

H Cliffbury Hotel

34 St David's Road,
Llandudno
LL30 2UH
Tel: (01492) 877224

HIGHLY COMMENDED

Non smoking, quietly situated in garden area. En-suites available. Colour TV, tea/coffee facilities, car parking, family rooms, good food, special diets. Close to beaches, shops, mountains, castles. Central heating. Access to rooms all day. High repeat clientele. Perfect for holiday, touring, walking, climbing. Personal attention at all times.

	SINGLE PER PERSON B&B		DOUBLE FOR 2 PERSONS B&B			🛏 9
						🛁 6
	MIN £	MAX £	MIN £	MAX £	OPEN	
	14.00	19.00	28.00	38.00	1-12	

H Seaclyffe Hotel

11 Church Walks,
Llandudno
LL30 2HG
Tel: (01492) 876803
Fax: (01492) 876803

A family run hotel with a warm and friendly atmosphere. Close to all amenities. 27 bedrooms, all en-suite with colour TV and tea/coffee makers. Sun lounge, pleasant garden, licensed bar, dance floor, entertainment 3 nights, heating in all rooms. Excellent home cooking with a varied choice of menu. Highly recommended.

	SINGLE PER PERSON B&B		DOUBLE FOR 2 PERSONS B&B			🛏 27
						🛁 27
	MIN £	MAX £	MIN £	MAX £	OPEN	
	17.50	18.50	35.00	37.00	3-12	

GH Winston Guest House

5 Church Walks,
Llandudno
LL30 2HD
Tel: (01492) 876144

COMMENDED

Family run for the past 24 years. 80 yards from the pier. Close to ski slope and shopping centre. Colour TV in all bedrooms, tea/coffee facilities provided. Excellent home cooked food with a varied menu, different diets catered for. Large comfortable lounge with colour television. No restrictions. AA Listed, QQQ.

	SINGLE PER PERSON B&B		DOUBLE FOR 2 PERSONS B&B			🛏 7
						🛁 7
	MIN £	MAX £	MIN £	MAX £	OPEN	
	16.50	17.50	33.00	34.00	1-12	

GH	Roughsedge Guest House

26-28 Marine Road,
Prestatyn
LL19 7HD
Tel: (01745) 887359
Fax: (01745) 887359

Family run establishment close to beaches, Pontins Presthaven Sands, Nova complex, golf, bowls and Offa's Dyke. Pleasant rooms, some en-suite, all with colour TV, tea/coffee facilities and clock radios. Home cooking, choice of menu, special diets, residential licence. Centrally heated, open lounge fire. Handy for rail and bus services and town centre. Children welcome. Credit cards accepted. AA.

P ⛄ 🛏	SINGLE PER PERSON B&B	DOUBLE FOR 2 PERSONS B&B	🛏 10
⛄ ✂ 🍴			🛏 3

MIN £	MAX £	MIN £	MAX £	OPEN
14.00	18.50	28.00	37.00	1-12

GH	St Winifreds Christian Guest House

Marine Drive,
Rhos on Sea
LL28 4NL
Tel: (01492) 544128

St Winifreds is situated on Marine Drive overlooking the sea, with views across the Bay of Colwyn. It is within easy access of Snowdonia. Special family reductions and pensioner weeks. Excellent food and a happy family atmosphere. Tea and coffee making facilities in each room.

P ⛄ ✂ 🍴	SINGLE PER PERSON B&B	DOUBLE FOR 2 PERSONS B&B	🛏 34
			🛏 -

MIN £	MAX £	MIN £	MAX £	OPEN
15.00	20.00	30.00	40.00	1-12

Call in at a Tourist Information Centre

Wales's network of TICs helps you get the best out of your holiday

* Information on what to see and where to go
* Local events
* Bed-booking service
* Brochures, maps and guides

It's so easy when you call in at a TIC

Great Orme Tramway, Llandudno

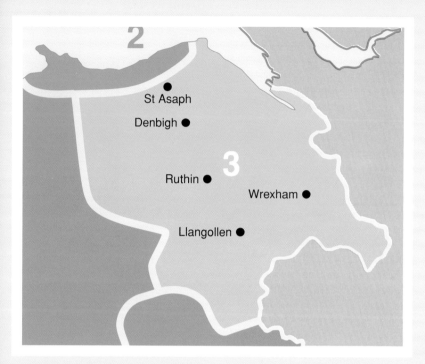

The North Wales Borderlands

Wales's border country is a mix of rolling green hills, lovely valleys, high moor and forest. The airy Clwydian Range guards the broad and fertile Vale of Clwyd – one of Wales's richest farming areas – which is dotted with historic towns. The valley around Llangollen is much deeper, its steep-sided hills rising to dramatic heights with names like 'World's End'. The wild moorlands above Denbigh are covered in heather and forest – and the waters of Llyn Brenig, a huge reservoir with many leisure facilities. There's much to see and do in this exhilarating area – walking, riding, canal cruising, and visiting places like Bodelwyddan Castle, where paintings from the National Portrait Gallery are exhibited, and Erddig, Wrexham, an unusual 'upstairs, downstairs' country house owned by the National Trust.

It's a fact...

The Clwydian Range of hills on the eastern flank of the Vale of Clwyd were designated an 'Area of Outstanding Natural Beauty' in 1985. Their summit, Moel Fammau, stands at 555m/1821ft. St Asaph has Britain's smallest cathedral. Llangollen's famous International Musical Eisteddfod was first held in 1947 to help bring countries together after war. Ruthin's medieval credentials are reinforced by the custom of the curfew bell, which is still rung at 8pm each night. Sir Henry Morton Stanley, who found Dr Livingstone in Africa, was born in Denbigh.

Ed1   Chirk   ⇌

Border town with famous castle which began life as a medieval fort and evolved into a splendid stately home. Good touring centre for the Vale of Llangollen, Clwydian Range and Mid Wales border country. Pontcysyllte Aqueduct, built by Thomas Telford, nearby.

Be7   Corwen

Pleasant market town in Vale of Edeyrnion. Livestock market held regularly. Fishing in River Dee, swimming pool, good walks. Well-located touring centre for Snowdonia and border country.

Be5   Denbigh

Castled town in Vale of Clwyd with much historic interest. Friary and museum. Pony trekking, riding, fishing, golf, tennis and bowls. Indoor heated swimming pool. Centrally located for enjoying the rolling hills of North-east Wales, a rich farming area full of attractive villages.

Cb4   Holywell

Place of pilgrimage for centuries, the 'Lourdes of Wales' with St Winefride's Holy Well. Remains of Basingwerk Abbey (1131) nearby. Leisure centre with swimming pools. Interesting and attractive Greenfield Valley Heritage Park.

Ec1   Llangollen

Romantic town on River Dee, famous for its International Musical Eisteddfod; singers and dancers from all over the world come here every July. The town's many attractions include a canal museum, pottery, weavers, ECTARC European Centre for Traditional and Regional Cultures and a standard-gauge steam railway. Plas Newydd (home of 'Ladies of Llangollen' fame) is nearby. Valle Crucis Abbey is 2 miles away in a superb setting and ruined Castell Dinas Brân overlooks the town. Browse through the town's little shops; stand on its 14th-century stone bridge; cruise along the canal. Golf course and wonderful walking in surrounding countryside.

Cb5   Mold

Town located on edge of the lovely Clwydian Range of hills. Excellent Theatr Clwyd offers wide range of entertainment. Visit Daniel Owen Centre, memorial to the 'Dickens of Wales'. Golf course. Loggerheads Country Park in wooded setting to the west. Good touring centre for country and coast.

Ca6   Ruthin

Attractive and historic market town noted for its fine architecture; curfew is still rung nightly. Many captivating old buildings. Medieval banquets in Ruthin Castle. Ancient St Peter's Church has beautiful gates and carved panels. Good range of small shops; craft centre with workshops. Ideal base for Vale of Clwyd.

Llangollen

Be4 St Asaph

Tiny city with the smallest cathedral in Britain, scene of the annual North Wales Music Festival. Prehistoric Cefn Caves nearby. Pleasantly situated on River Elwy in verdant Vale of Clwyd. Three important historic sites on doorstep – medieval Rhuddlan Castle, Bodelwyddan Castle (with noted art collection) and Bodrhyddan Hall.

Cc6 Wrexham

Busy industrial and commercial town, gateway to North Wales. St Giles's Church has graceful tower and altar piece given by Elihu Yale of Yale University fame (his tomb is in the churchyard). Visit Erddig Hall, an unusual country house on outskirts, and the Clywedog Valley Heritage Park. Good shopping and excellent little heritage centre. Industrial museum at neighbouring Bersham. Art gallery, swimming pool, golf.

Erddig Hall near Wrexham

Chirk Corwen Denbigh Holywell Llangollen

GH | Bryn Haul

Castle Road,
Chirk, Wrexham
LL14 5BS
Tel: (01691) 772698

 AWAITING INSPECTION

Country house in quiet location, set in large gardens. Close to Chirk Castle, Offa's Dyke, the Ceiriog Valley and Berwyn Mountains. Golf, fishing and pony trekking nearby.

i

P C	♘ ⌷	SINGLE PER PERSON B&B		DOUBLE FOR 2 PERSONS B&B		🛏 3 🛏 1
		MIN £	MAX £	MIN £	MAX £	OPEN
		16.50	-	33.00	-	1-12

GH | Powys House Estate

Bonwm,
Corwen
LL21 9EG
Tel: (01490) 412367

  HIGHLY COMMENDED AWARD ♛ ♛♛

Country house only 9 miles from Llangollen, set in large gardens with swimming pool and tennis court. Spacious, well furnished en-suite bedrooms all with colour TV, hairdryer, beverage making facilities. Large guest lounge with log burning stove. Friendly, relaxed atmosphere. Ideal touring base. Full brochure on request. Self-catering cottages also available.

i

P ⌫	⌷ ⟘⌑	SINGLE PER PERSON B&B		DOUBLE FOR 2 PERSONS B&B		🛏 3 🛏 3
		MIN £	MAX £	MIN £	MAX £	OPEN
		22.00	23.00	34.00	36.00	1-12

H | Abbey Grange Hotel

Horseshoe Pass Road,
Llangollen
LL20 8DD
Tel: (01978) 860753

 ♛ ♛♛

Just 1.5 miles from Llangollen, Abbey Grange is an ideal base for walking holidays or for touring North Wales with coastal resorts and Snowdonia National Park less than an hour's drive away. Food and drink are served all day and comfort is assured with relaxed, friendly service. Open log fire in the winter.

i

P ♙ ⟘ ⌑ ⌷	SINGLE PER PERSON B&B		DOUBLE FOR 2 PERSONS B&B		🛏 8 🛏 8
	MIN £	MAX £	MIN £	MAX £	OPEN
	18.00	20.00	32.00	36.00	1-12

H | Central Hotel

Holyhead Road,
Corwen, Nr Llangollen
LL21 0DE
Tel: (01490) 412462

 ♛ ♛♛

For all year round holidays and short breaks. A warm welcome and excellent cuisine await you. Situated at the foot of the Berwyn Mountains on a bend of the beautiful River Dee, it is the perfect centre for walking, sightseeing, a gateway to the "wilds of North Wales" and central to Llangollen, Ruthin and Bala. Pets by arrangement.

i

P C ⌑ ⌷ ⟘	♙ ⟘ ⌑	SINGLE PER PERSON B&B		DOUBLE FOR 2 PERSONS B&B		🛏 10 🛏 10
		MIN £	MAX £	MIN £	MAX £	OPEN
		17.50	20.00	-	40.00	1-12

GH | Cayo Guest House

74 Vale Street,
Denbigh
LL16 3BW
Tel: (01745) 812686

♛ ♛♛

Long established, centrally situated guest house. Guests have access at all times. Most rooms en-suite. Well behaved dogs welcome. Good food using local produce, special menu on request. Ideal for touring North Wales, excellent area for golf, gliding, angling and walking. AA, QQQQ.

i

♙ ⟑	⌷ ⌑	SINGLE PER PERSON B&B		DOUBLE FOR 2 PERSONS B&B		🛏 5 🛏 4
		MIN £	MAX £	MIN £	MAX £	OPEN
		16.00	17.00	32.00	34.00	1-12

GH | Bryn Hyfryd Guest House

Llantysilio,
Llangollen
LL20 7YU
Tel: (01978) 860011

♛ ♛♛

Bryn Hyfryd is situated in the tiny hamlet of Llantysilio. All room have magnificent views over Dee Valley and are equipped with private bathroom, TV and drink making facilities. Lovely walks can be taken. Llangollen Steam Railway, Canal Museum and many attractions just 2.5 miles away. Stroll to 16th century inn.

i

P C ⟑	♙ ⌷	SINGLE PER PERSON B&B		DOUBLE FOR 2 PERSONS B&B		🛏 3 🛏 3
		MIN £	MAX £	MIN £	MAX £	OPEN
		-	16.00	-	30.00	1-11

GH | Corwen Court Private Hotel

London Road,
Corwen
LL21 0DP
Tel: (01490) 412854

♛ ♛♛

Situated on the A5. Converted old Police Station and Courthouse. Six prisoners' cells now single bedrooms, hot and cold water in each. Three only sharing a bathroom. Double bedrooms have en-suite bathroom. Comfortable lounge, colour TV, dining room with separate tables where magistrates once presided. Centrally heated. Fire certificate. Convenient base for touring North Wales.

i

♙ ⌑ ⟘ ⌷	SINGLE PER PERSON B&B		DOUBLE FOR 2 PERSONS B&B		🛏 10 🛏 4
	MIN £	MAX £	MIN £	MAX £	OPEN
	13.00	14.00	28.00	30.00	3-11

FH | Greenhill Farm

Bryn Celyn,
Holywell
CH8 7QF
Tel: (01352) 713270

 ♛ ♛♛

Our 15th century timber framed farmhouse overlooks the Dee estuary. Modernised to include one family room (en-suite), twin and double rooms all with tea/coffee making and colour TV's. Comfortable oak beamed lounge and panelled dining room. Games/utility room with snooker table and washing machine. Children are made especially welcome.

i

P ⌑ ⌷	SINGLE PER PERSON B&B		DOUBLE FOR 2 PERSONS B&B		🛏 3 🛏 1
	MIN £	MAX £	MIN £	MAX £	OPEN
	16.00	-	32.00	-	3-10

GH | Glanafon Guest House

Abbey Road,
Llangollen
LL20 8SS
Tel: (01978) 860725

♛ ♛♛

Friendly, family run, Victorian guest house overlooking River Dee and near the Eisteddfod Field. Spacious, comfortable room which is a double, twin or family. Colour TV and guests' own bathroom. Children welcome. Ideally situated for fishing, canoeing, walking, touring. Six minutes' stroll to town centre along the canal towpath.

i

P ⟑ ⌑ ⌫	SINGLE PER PERSON B&B		DOUBLE FOR 2 PERSONS B&B		🛏 1 🛏 1
	MIN £	MAX £	MIN £	MAX £	OPEN
	-	-	30.00	32.00	1-12

Llangollen Mold Ruthin St Asaph Wrexham

GH	The Grange

Grange Road,
Llangollen
LL20 8AP
Tel: (01978) 860366

HIGHLY COMMENDED

An attractive country house of character situated in town within a tranquil and secluded 2 acre garden. Spacious and comfortable twin, double or family bedrooms, all en-suite with tea/coffee facilities and central heating. Child reductions and cot available. Interesting beamed lounge with TV. Parking in grounds. Vegetarians catered for.

P ⬛ 🚲	SINGLE PER PERSON B&B	DOUBLE FOR 2 PERSONS B&B	🛏 3 🛏 3
	MIN £ -	MAX £ -	MIN £ 35.00	MAX £ 35.00	OPEN 1-12

GH	Eyarth Station

Llanfair Dyffryn Clwyd,
Ruthin
LL15 2EE
Tel: (01824) 703643
Fax: (01824) 707464

AWARD HIGHLY COMMENDED

Former railway station, now a superbly converted country house. Six bedrooms, all en-suite with shower. TV lounge, swimming pool, car park, magnificent views. Located in beautiful countryside, only 3 minutes drive to Ruthin Castle's medieval banquets and town. Centre for Chester, Snowdonia, Llangollen, Bala and coast. Home cooking. Credit cards accepted. Listen to our local Welsh choir. BTA Commended. AA Merit Awards.

P 🍴 ⬛ 🚲 🍽	SINGLE PER PERSON B&B	DOUBLE FOR 2 PERSONS B&B	🛏 6 🛏 6
	MIN £ -	MAX £ -	MIN £ 40.00	MAX £ 40.00	OPEN 1-12

GH	Plas Uchaf

Graigadwywynt,
Llanfair Dyffryn Clwyd,
Ruthin LL15 2TF
Tel: (01824) 705794

HIGHLY COMMENDED

16th century manor house set in beautiful countryside of historical interest. Wealth of beams, panelling and log fires. Tastefully decorated and furnished. All rooms with en-suite facilities, TV and tea making facilities. Centrally situated for Snowdonia, Llangollen and Chester. A warm welcome is assured with a Welsh speaking family.

P 🍴 ⬛	SINGLE PER PERSON B&B	DOUBLE FOR 2 PERSONS B&B	🛏 3 🛏 3
	MIN £ 16.00	MAX £ 18.00	MIN £ 28.00	MAX £ 33.00	OPEN 1-12

FH	Tyn Celyn Farmhouse

Tyndwr,
Llangollen
LL20 8AR
Tel: (01978) 861117

Spacious oak beamed farmhouse on the outskirts of Llangollen. Situated in a peaceful valley with beautiful views. All bedrooms have en-suite bathrooms, beverage tray, television and central heating. Ideally situated for walking, golf, horse riding, and for visiting Snowdonia, North Wales coast and Chester. Just 1.5 miles from Llangollen town centre. Ample secure parking.

P ⬛ 🚭	SINGLE PER PERSON B&B	DOUBLE FOR 2 PERSONS B&B	🛏 3 🛏 3
	MIN £ -	MAX £ -	MIN £ 35.00	MAX £ 38.00	OPEN 1-12

GH	Gorffwysfa

Llanfair Dyffryn Clwyd,
Ruthin
LL15 2UN
Tel: (01824) 702432

COMMENDED

"Gorffwysfa" resting place. Situated at the foot of Offa's Dyke and the Clwydian Range. Spacious en-suite accommodation in large Victorian country house 5 minutes from the medieval town of Ruthin. Ideal for exploring Chester, Snowdonia and North Wales with its castles, gardens, National Trust properties and seaside resorts. Special rates for families and longer stays.

P 🐕	SINGLE PER PERSON B&B	DOUBLE FOR 2 PERSONS B&B	🛏 3 🛏 3
C ⬛ 🚫 🍽	MIN £ -	MAX £ 16.00	MIN £ -	MAX £ 32.00	OPEN 1-12

FH	Plas Penucha

Caerwys,
Mold
CH7 5BH
Tel: (01352) 720210

HIGHLY COMMENDED

Welcome to this 16th century farmhouse, altered over succeeding generations but retaining history and serenity in comfortable surroundings. Extensive gardens overlooking Clwydian Hills. Spacious lounge with extensive library. Four well equipped bedrooms, 2 en-suite. Full central heating, log fires. 2 miles A55 Expressway, ideal touring centre for North Wales and Chester. Brochure from Nest Price.

P 🐕	SINGLE PER PERSON B&B	DOUBLE FOR 2 PERSONS B&B	🛏 4 🛏 2
C ⬛ 🚫 🍽	MIN £ 17.50	MAX £ 17.50	MIN £ 35.00	MAX £ 35.00	OPEN 1-12

FH	Maes Garmon Farm

Off Gwernaffield Road,
Gwernaffield,
Mold CH7 5DB
Tel: (01352) 759887

HIGHLY COMMENDED

Imagine a peaceful secluded valley; a converted stable adjoining a 17th century farmhouse; a welcome of tea and scones; accommodation of the highest standard; a wealth of beams, antiques, oak and pine furnishings. Guests' own lounge, pretty en-suite bedrooms, two double, one twin. Beautiful three acre garden, summerhouse, pond and stream. Convenient for Chester and Snowdonia.

P 🚫 🍽	SINGLE PER PERSON B&B	DOUBLE FOR 2 PERSONS B&B	🛏 3 🛏 3
	MIN £ 18.00	MAX £ 20.00	MIN £ 32.00	MAX £ 36.00	OPEN 1-12

GH	The Old Rectory

Clocaenog,
Ruthin
LL15 2AT
Tel: (01824) 750740

We welcome guests who can share our spacious Georgian home in peaceful countryside just 10 minutes' drive from Ruthin. Three bedrooms, en-suite or with private bathroom. Centrally heated throughout. The visitors' lounge has colour TV, radio and many books for your enjoyment. Explore Snowdonia or visit Llangollen and Chester which are all within less than an hour's drive.

P C	SINGLE PER PERSON B&B	DOUBLE FOR 2 PERSONS B&B	🛏 3 🛏 3
⬛ 🚫	MIN £ 15.00	MAX £ 17.00	MIN £ 30.00	MAX £ 34.00	OPEN 1-12

GH	Mill House

Higher Wych,
Malpas,
Cheshire SY14 7JR
Tel: (01948) 780362
Fax: (01948) 780566

HIGHLY COMMENDED

A converted mill house in a quiet valley on the Wales/England border. One double with en-suite shower and WC, one twin bedded room, tea/coffee making facilities. Lounge with TV and open log fire. Reduced rates for children and senior citizens. Within easy reach of Llangollen, Chester, Shrewsbury and Wrexham.

P ⬛ 🍽	SINGLE PER PERSON B&B	DOUBLE FOR 2 PERSONS B&B	🛏 2 🛏 1
	MIN £ 16.00	MAX £ 16.00	MIN £ 32.00	MAX £ 32.00	OPEN 1-11

This part of Wales takes its name from the jagged pinnacle of Snowdon. Yet the

Snowdonia National Park extends southwards for hundreds of square miles from Snowdon itself, all the way to Dolgellau and beyond, and eastwards to Bala. All of Wales's high and mighty mountains are here – Tryfan, the Glyders, the Carneddau, the

Aran and Arennigs, and Cader Idris. Snowdonia, a place of surprising scenic variety, also has its oakwood vales, its forested hills, its lakes and rivers, its brooding moorlands. Mountains sweep down to the sea along a beautiful coastline of sandy beaches and estuaries. And along the Llŷn Peninsula – 'Snowdonia's arm' – you'll find some of the wildest coastal scenery in Britain as well as sheltered beaches and picturesque little resorts.

It's a fact…

The Snowdonia National Park covers 838 square miles. It was Wales's first national park, designated in 1951. Snowdonia's Welsh name is *Eryri*, which means 'the mountain of the eagles'. The peak of Snowdon stands at 1085m/3560ft, the highest mountain in England and Wales. The Llŷn Peninsula has the highest percentage of Welsh speakers in Wales (75%). Llŷn was declared an 'Area of Outstanding Natural Beauty' in 1956. Bwlch y Groes, the mountain road between Dinas Mawddwy and Bala, is Wales's highest road, climbing to 546m/1791ft. Bala Lake is Wales's largest natural lake.

Db5   Abergynolwyn

Attractively located former slate quarrying village surrounded by forests and the green foothills of Cader Idris. Narrow-gauge Talyllyn Railway runs almost to the village from Tywyn. Good choice of local walks. Visit Tal-y-llyn Lake, Bird Rock and atmospheric Castell-y-Bere.

Ac5   Abersoch

Dinghy sailing and windsurfing centre with sandy beaches. Superb coastal scenery with easy walks. Pony trekking, golf, fishing and sea trips. Llanengan's historic church nearby.

De2   Bala

Traditional Welsh country town with tree-lined main street and interesting little shops. Narrow-gauge railway runs one side of Bala Lake, 4 miles long (the largest natural lake in Wales) and ringed with mountains. Golf, sailing, fishing, canoeing – a natural touring centre for Snowdonia.

Ae3   Bangor

Compact cathedral city of character overlooking the Menai Strait; gateway to Anglesey and Snowdonia's Ogwen Valley, with university college and 6th-century cathedral. Attractions include Theatr Gwynedd, Penrhyn Castle, museum and art gallery and an exquisitely renovated pier. Heated swimming pool, yachting and fishing.

Db4   Barmouth

Superbly located resort at the mouth of lovely Mawddach Estuary. Golden sands, miles of wonderful mountain and estuary walks nearby. Promenade, funfair, harbour and pony rides on the beach. Lifeboat and Shipwreck Centre museums. Good shops and inns. Excellent parking on seafront.

Ae6   Beddgelert

Village romantically set amid glorious mountain scenery, with Nant Gwynant Valley to the east and rocky Aberglaslyn Pass to the south. Snowdonia's grandeur all around; Wordsworth made a famous dawn ascent of Mount Snowdon from here. Marvellous walks; links with legendary dog named Gelert. Visit Sygun Copper Mine and Cae Du Farm Park, two nearby attractions.

Bb6   Betws-y-Coed

Wooded village and popular mountain resort in picturesque setting where three rivers meet. Good touring centre, close to best mountain area of Snowdonia. Tumbling rivers and waterfalls emerge from a tangle of treetops. Trout fishing, craft shops, golf course, railway and motor museums, Snowdonia National Park Visitor Centre. Nature trails very popular with hikers. Swallow Falls a 'must'.

Ba7   Blaenau Ffestiniog

One-time centre of the Welsh slate industry, now a tourist town with two cavernous slate quarries – Llechwedd and Gloddfa Ganol – open to visitors. Narrow-gauge Ffestiniog Railway runs from Porthmadog. Nearby Stwlan Dam, part of hydro-electric scheme, reached through marvellous mountain scenery. Visitor centre explains how electricity is generated.

Ad4   Caernarfon

Dominated by magnificent 13th-century castle, most famous of Wales's medieval fortresses. Many museums in castle, maritime museum in town. Caernarfon Air World at Dinas Dinlle, Segontium Roman Fort and Museum on hill above town. Popular sailing centre, old harbour, market square, Lloyd George statue. Holiday centre at gateway of Snowdonia. Parc Glynllifon nearby.

Ba6   Capel Curig

Village ringed by Snowdonia's highest mountains. Great favourite with climbers. Good walking and fishing. Craft shops.

Bb4   Conwy   🚆

Historic town with mighty castle and complete ring of medieval town walls. Dramatic estuary setting. Many ancient buildings including Aberconwy House. Telford Suspension Bridge, popular fish quay, spectacular wall walks. Golf, pony trekking, Butterfly House, aquarium, pleasure cruises. Tiny 'smallest house' on quay. Touring centre for Snowdonia.

Dc5   Corris

Village in the foothills of Cader Idris mountain range. Excellent craft centre and exciting King Arthur's Labyrinth attraction. Small railway museum. Centre for Alternative Technology, the 'village of the future', close by.

Be7   Corwen

Pleasant market town in Vale of Edeyrnion. Livestock market held regularly. Fishing in River Dee, swimming pool, good walks. Well-located touring centre for Snowdonia and border country.

Ad7   Criccieth   🚆

Ideal family resort with good beach. Romantic ruined castle on headland overlooking sea. Salmon and trout in nearby rivers and lakes. Festival of Music and the Arts in June. Village of Llanystumdwy with Lloyd George Museum nearby.

Dd4   Dinas Mawddwy

Mountain village famed for its salmon and trout fishing and marvellous walks. On fringes of Snowdonia National Park. Visit the extensive Meirion Woollen Mill with craft shop, tea shop. Drive over the spectacular Bwlch y Groes mountain road to Bala, the highest road in Wales.

Dc4   Dolgellau

Handsome stone-built market town which seems to have grown naturally out of the mountains. The heights of Cader Idris loom above the rooftops. Interesting shops, pubs, cafes. Museum of the Quakers in town centre. Visit a gold mine in nearby forest. Excellent base for touring the coast and countryside.

Db4   Fairbourne   🚆

Quiet resort with 2 miles of sand south of Mawddach Estuary. Railway buffs travel far to ride on its 1' 3" gauge Fairbourne and Barmouth Steam Railway.

Da2   Harlech   🚆

Small, stone-built town dominated by remains of 13th-century castle – site of Owain Glyndŵr's last stand. Dramatically set on a high crag, the castle commands a magnificent panorama of rolling sand dunes, sea and mountains. Home of the 18-hole Royal St David's Golf Club. Shell Island nearby. Theatre and swimming pool. Visitors can explore the chambers of the Old Llanfair Slate Caverns just south of Harlech.

Bb5   Llanbedr-y-Cennin

Village on western flank of lovely Vale of Conwy between Llanrwst and coast. Splendid views from ancient hillfort in hills above. Woollen mill and Roman spa at nearby Trefriw.

Ae4 Llanberis

Popular centre for walkers and climbers, least difficult (5 miles) walk to Snowdon summit starts here. For easy ride up take Snowdon Mountain Railway. Many things to see and do in this lively mountain town – Llanberis Lake Railway, slate industry museum. Power of Wales interpretive centre with unforgettable trip to the awesome tunnels of the Dinorwig Hydro-Electric Scheme, activity-packed Padarn Country Park, ancient Dolbadarn Castle, Bryn Brâs Castle at nearby Llanrug.

Bb6 Llanrwst ⇌

Attractive town where the crystal-clear River Conwy runs through lush meadows; chief shopping centre of upper Conwy Valley. Handsome bridge designed by Inigo Jones in 1636. Gwydir Park has bowling, putting and children's playground. Charming Gwydir Uchaf Chapel and scenic Llyn Geirionydd in woodlands above town. Gwydir Castle open to the public. Bodnant Garden 8 miles away.

Dc5 Machynlleth ⇌

Historic market town near beautiful Dovey Estuary. Owain Glyndŵr's Parliament House in the wide handsome main street is now a museum and brass rubbing centre. Superbly equipped Bro Dyfi Leisure Centre offers wide range of activities. Celtica centre tells the story of Celtic myth and legend. Ancient and modern meet here; the inventive Centre for Alternative Technology is 3 miles away, just off the A487 to Dolgellau. Felin Crewi Flour Mill is off the A489 2 miles to the east.

Ae7 Porthmadog ⇌

Harbour town and shopping centre named after William Madocks, who built mile-long Cob embankment. Steam narrow-gauge Ffestiniog Railway runs to Blaenau Ffestiniog, with its slate caverns. Also Welsh Highland Railway. Pottery, maritime museum, car museum. Portmeirion Italianate village and good beaches nearby.

Dc5 Tal-y-llyn

Lakeside village in magnificent setting below Cader Idris mountain, ideally placed for fishing and walking. Narrow-gauge Talyllyn Railway, which runs to a nearby halt, connects with Tywyn.

Da6 Tywyn ⇌

Seaside resort on Cardigan Bay, with beach activities, sea and river fishing and golf among its leading attractions. Good leisure centre. Narrow-gauge Talyllyn Railway runs inland from here and St Cadfan's Stone and Llanegryn Church are important Christian monuments. In the hills stands Castell-y-Bere, a native Welsh castle, and Bird Rock, a haven for birdlife.

Snowdon Mountain Railway

FH | Tanycoed Ucha

Abergynolwyn,
Tywyn
LL36 9UP
Tel: (01654) 782228

Come and stay and enjoy a quite holiday on our mixed working farm. Farmhouse over a hundred years old. Modernised for comfort. Twin, double and single bedrooms, bathroom, tea and coffee facilities in bedrooms. 600 yards off B4405, Tywyn 6 miles, Dolgellau 14 miles. The Talyllyn Narrow Gauge Railway runs through our land. Dolgoch Falls 1 mile away.

P 🐕 🍴	SINGLE PER PERSON B&B	DOUBLE FOR 2 PERSONS B&B	🛏 3 🛁 -
	MIN £	MAX £	MIN £	MAX £	OPEN
	13.50	14.00	27.00	28.00	3-11

GH | Frondderw Private Hotel

Stryd-y-Fron,
Bala
LL23 7YD
Tel: (01678) 520301

COMMENDED

Charming period mansion quietly situated on hillside overlooking Bala town and lake with magnificent views of Berwyn Mountains. All rooms have hot and cold, central heating, tea/coffee making facilities. Lounge, separate TV lounge with colour TV, ample parking. Dinner optional, vegetarians catered for. Licensed. Ideal centre for touring, walking, water sports. Concessionary golf.

P 🍴	SINGLE PER PERSON B&B	DOUBLE FOR 2 PERSONS B&B	🛏 8 🛁 4
	MIN £	MAX £	MIN £	MAX £	OPEN
	15.00	-	30.00	-	3-11

FH | Cwm Hwylfod

Cefn ddwysarn,
Bala
LL23 7LN
Tel: (01678) 530310

COMMENDED

Near Bala, 400 year old farmhouse on working farm. Spectacular views, friendly atmosphere. Children welcome. Guest lounge. Central heating. Home cooking a speciality. B&B, evening meal optional, 01678 530310

P 🐕 🍴	SINGLE PER PERSON B&B	DOUBLE FOR 2 PERSONS B&B	🛏 3 🛁 -
	MIN £	MAX £	MIN £	MAX £	OPEN
	14.00	16.00	28.00	32.00	1-12

GH | Llysfor Guest House

Abersoch,
Near Pwllheli
LL53 7AL
Tel: (01758) 712248

COMMENDED

A well established family run guest house, our aim is to please and make your stay enjoyable. Hot and cold water, shaver points, tea/coffee facilities in all bedrooms. Some en-suite rooms. Comfortable dining room, separate lounge with TV. One minute to beach, overlooking harbour. Private parking, own grounds. Fire certificate. Reduced rates for children. Enquiries Mr A. Hiorns.

P 🐕	SINGLE PER PERSON B&B	DOUBLE FOR 2 PERSONS B&B	🛏 8 🛁 2
	MIN £	MAX £	MIN £	MAX £	OPEN
	13.50	15.50	31.00	35.00	4-10

GH | Plas Gower

Llangower,
Near Bala
LL23 7BY
Tel: (01678) 520431
Fax: (01678) 520431

HIGHLY COMMENDED

Welcoming Georgian stone house with beautiful views over Bala Lake and surrounding mountains. The lakeshore is only 2 minutes' walk away. Peaceful, relaxed atmosphere, log fires, lovely garden. Ideal for walking, sailing or exploring the delights of Mid and North Wales. Many eating places in Bala, 2.5 miles away.

P 🏠 ✂	SINGLE PER PERSON B&B	DOUBLE FOR 2 PERSONS B&B	🛏 2 🛁 1
	MIN £	MAX £	MIN £	MAX £	OPEN
	17.50	18.50	35.00	37.00	1-12

FH | Eirianfa Farm

Sarnau,
Bala
LL23 7LH
Tel: (01678) 530389

Comfortable modern farmhouse 3 miles NE Bala on A494 overlooking the lovely Berwyn mountains and Cader Idris. Ideal centre for touring Mid and North Wales. All bedrooms with hot and cold, central heating and tea/coffee making facilities. Good centre for walking. Sailing and windsurfing on Bala Lake. Also canoeing on River Tryweryn. Working farm with private lake for fishing.

P 🏠 🍴	SINGLE PER PERSON B&B	DOUBLE FOR 2 PERSONS B&B	🛏 3 🛁 1
	MIN £	MAX £	MIN £	MAX £	OPEN
	13.50	17.00	-	-	1-12

GH | Bronwylfa Guest House

Llandderfel,
Bala
LL23 7HG
Tel: (01678) 530207/530395

DELUXE

Victorian country house and coach house, tranquil setting, Berwyn mountain view. 4 miles from Bala, 6 miles off A5, edge of farmland and excellent base for touring Snowdonia National Park. Watersports or walking. Large en-suite bedrooms (2 families), colour TV, beverage trays, home cooking, warm welcome assured. Relax and unwind in conservatory with tea and cakes. Private grounds with large parking. Non smokers preferred please.

P C 🏠 🍴	SINGLE PER PERSON B&B	DOUBLE FOR 2 PERSONS B&B	🛏 4 🛁 3
	MIN £	MAX £	MIN £	MAX £	OPEN
	18.00	20.00	32.00	38.00	1-12

GH | Trem Aran House

1 Glannau Tegid,
Tegid Street,
Bala
LL23 7NZ
Tel: (01678) 520848

AWARD

Two bedrooms with wash hand basins. Two private baths. Large guest lounge. Large garden.

P 🐕 🏠 ✂ 🍴	SINGLE PER PERSON B&B	DOUBLE FOR 2 PERSONS B&B	🛏 2 🛁 -
	MIN £	MAX £	MIN £	MAX £	OPEN
	14.00	-	-	28.00	1-12

FH | Erw Feurig Farm Guest House

Cefnddwysarn,
Bala
LL23 7LL
Tel: (01678) 530262

HIGHLY COMMENDED

Beautifully situated, the farm guest house is the perfect centre for sightseeing and walking. Double, twin and family rooms, two en-suite. Excellent meals served in pleasant dining room. Separate TV lounge. tea/coffee trays in all rooms. Private fishing lake. Be sure of a real Welsh welcome at Erw Feurig. Fire certificate held.

P 🏠 ✂ 🍴	SINGLE PER PERSON B&B	DOUBLE FOR 2 PERSONS B&B	🛏 4 🛁 2
	MIN £	MAX £	MIN £	MAX £	OPEN
	16.00	-	-	33.00	1-12

Bala Bangor Barmouth

FH	Rhydydefaid Farm

Frongoch,
Bala
LL23 7NT
Tel: (01678) 520456
Fax: (01678) 520456

HIGHLY COMMENDED

Traditional Welsh stone farmhouse on 100 acres working farm. Three miles from Bala. Oak beams and inglenook. Choice of double, twin, family rooms with central heating, some with en-suite facilities. Beverage trays, wholesome Welsh breakfast and hospitality. Near National White Water Centre. Excellent base for touring Snowdonia mountains and coast. Brochure from Mrs Davies. ℹ

	SINGLE PER PERSON B&B	DOUBLE FOR 2 PERSONS B&B		🛏 3
				🛁 2

MIN £	MAX £	MIN £	MAX £	OPEN
15.00	17.00	28.00	34.00	1-12

H	Eryl Môr Hotel

2 Upper Garth Road,
Bangor
LL57 2SR
Tel: (01248) 353789/354042
Fax: (01248) 354042

HIGHLY COMMENDED

Small family run hotel with splendid views of the Victorian pier, Menai Strait and Snowdonia. Restaurant and bar menus, good vegetarian and children's choice, fully licensed. All rooms have colour TV, direct dial telephone, tea and coffee facilities; sea views can be reserved. Competitive rates, short breaks, weekly rates. Call for our brochure 01248 353789. ℹ

	SINGLE PER PERSON B&B	DOUBLE FOR 2 PERSONS B&B		🛏 24
				🛁 16

MIN £	MAX £	MIN £	MAX £	OPEN
15.00	20.00	30.00	34.00	1-12

GH	Yr-Elen

Bryn, Llandegai,
Bangor
LL57 4LD
Tel: (01248) 364591

Set in beautiful countryside, within walking distance of National Trust's Penrhyn Castle. Panoramic views of Snowdonia and sea. Perfectly situated for Anglesey, Gwynedd, Irish Sea crossing. Ground floor bedrooms with colour TV, teasmade, washbasin, adjacent bathroom sole use of guests. Garden. Parking. A5122 off A5/A55. Guests' comments - "exceptional value", "superior", "homely B&B". ℹ

	SINGLE PER PERSON B&B	DOUBLE FOR 2 PERSONS B&B		🛏 2
				-

MIN £	MAX £	MIN £	MAX £	OPEN
-	-	26.00	26.00	3-11

FH	Tai'r Felin Farm

Frongoch,
Bala
LL23 7NS
Tel: (01678) 520763

COMMENDED

Situated three miles from Bala, A4212 & B4501 roads, within the Snowdonia National Park. Double and twin bedrooms, H & C, tea/coffee facilities, clock radio, bathroom with shower. Lounge with colour TV, log fire, separate tables in dining room. Recommended for excellent cooking and warm friendly atmosphere. Ideal base for touring Mid and North Wales. Relax and enjoy a homely welcome. Contact Mrs C Morris. ℹ

	SINGLE PER PERSON B&B	DOUBLE FOR 2 PERSONS B&B		🛏 2
				-

MIN £	MAX £	MIN £	MAX £	OPEN
15.00	16.00	28.00	32.00	3-10

GH	Nant y Fedw

Trefelin, Llandegai,
Near Bangor
LL57 4LH
Tel: (01248) 351683

B&B in charming beamed country cottage situated in countryside between the mountains of Snowdonia and the sea. All rooms have private bathroom, tea and coffee making facilities, colour TV, radio alarm clock, hairdryer and keys. Convenient for all areas of North Wales and Anglesey. ℹ

	SINGLE PER PERSON B&B	DOUBLE FOR 2 PERSONS B&B		🛏 2
				🛁 2

MIN £	MAX £	MIN £	MAX £	OPEN
18.00	18.00	30.00	30.00	1-12

FH	Goetre Isaf Farmhouse

Caernarfon Road,
Bangor
LL57 4DB
Tel: (01248) 364541
Fax: (01248) 364541

COMMENDED

Superb country situation with ,magnificent views. Although isolated, only 2 miles (3 Km) from Bangor mainline station. Ideal touring centre for the mountains of Snowdonia, Isle of Anglesey, and the beaches of the Llŷn Peninsula. Imaginative farmhouse cooking. Special diets accommodated and vegetarians welcome. All bedrooms with dial-phone facilities. Stabling by arrangement. ℹ

	SINGLE PER PERSON B&B	DOUBLE FOR 2 PERSONS B&B		🛏 3
				🛁 1

MIN £	MAX £	MIN £	MAX £	OPEN
15.00	-	26.00	-	1-12

H	The British Hotel

High Street,
Bangor
LL57 1NP
Tel: (01248) 364911

COMMENDED

Bangor's largest hotel, within easy reach of Anglesey, Snowdonia and Holyhead sea link to Ireland. Golf, sailing, swimming pool available nearby. The hotel has conference facilities, comfortable lounges, cocktail and buttery bar, dining room, carvery, car park, night porter. Lift to en-suite bedrooms. All with colour TV, hospitality tray, direct dial telephone. ℹ

	SINGLE PER PERSON B&B	DOUBLE FOR 2 PERSONS B&B		🛏 49
				🛁 49

MIN £	MAX £	MIN £	MAX £	OPEN
13.00	20.00	26.00	40.00	1-12

GH	Rainbow Court

Village Square,
Pentir, Near Bangor
LL57 4UY
Tel: (01248) 353099
Fax: (01248) 353099

Quiet village location within easy reach of A5/A55. Riding, walking, golf, water sports, castles, attractions, mountains. Superb views. A la carte breakfast, evening restaurant serving table d'hôte, à la carte, connoisseur and vegetarian menus. Property converted post office situated in a village full of history, potted local history available. Pleasant homely atmosphere in total non smoking establishment. ℹ

	SINGLE PER PERSON B&B	DOUBLE FOR 2 PERSONS B&B		🛏 2
				🛁 2

MIN £	MAX £	MIN £	MAX £	OPEN
-	-	13.00	17.00	1-12

GH	Pen Parc Guest House

Park Road,
Barmouth
LL42 1PH
Tel: (01341) 280150

HIGHLY COMMENDED

A Victorian manse in quiet situation overlooking park, yet only four minutes from sea. Hot and cold water and tea making facilities in all rooms. All bedrooms on first floor. We pride ourselves on personal service and good food, with traditional and vegetarian cuisine and special diets. TV lounge. Walkers welcome. Sorry, no young children or pets. ℹ

	SINGLE PER PERSON B&B	DOUBLE FOR 2 PERSONS B&B		🛏 4
				🛁

MIN £	MAX £	MIN £	MAX £	OPEN
14.50	15.00	29.00	30.00	3-10

GH | The Sandpiper

7 Marine Parade,
Barmouth
LL42 1NA
Tel: (01341) 280318

 HIGHLY COMMENDED

Situated on Barmouth seafront. The Sandpiper is owned by Susan and John Palmer who, as keen walkers, can offer local advice. There is parking outside and the station is a a short level walk. Most double rooms have en-suite facilities including a ground floor bedroom. All rooms have television and free tea/coffee. No pets.

		SINGLE PER PERSON B&B	DOUBLE FOR 2 PERSONS B&B	🛏 11 / 🛁 6
MIN £	MAX £	MIN £	MAX £	OPEN
14.00	15.00	25.00	33.00	3-10

H | Swallow Falls Hotel

Betws-y-Coed
LL27 0DW
Tel: (01690) 710796
Fax: (01690) 710191

 COMMENDED

Situated just outside the picturesque village of Betws-y-Coed in the beautiful Snowdonia National Park nestling between the mountains and the sea. The hotel has 10 en-suite bedrooms and two licensed bars offering delicious home cooked food. Ideal base for walking and climbing! Don't miss our unique Welsh fudge pantry, see demonstrations and enjoy free tasting.

		SINGLE PER PERSON B&B	DOUBLE FOR 2 PERSONS B&B	🛏 10 / 🛁 10
MIN £	MAX £	MIN £	MAX £	OPEN
-	-	40.00	40.00	1-12

GH | Bryn Llewelyn Guest House

Holyhead Road,
Betws-y-Coed
LL24 0BN
Tel: (01690) 710601

 COMMENDED

Welcome to Betws-y-Coed. Bryn Llewelyn is a beautiful Victorian house near the centre of this scenic Snowdonia village. Restaurants, shops, riverside and forest walks close to our doorstep. Within easy reach of mountains. Comfortable rooms with central heating, tea/coffee, TV on request. Guests' lounge, large car park. AA and RAC recommended.

		SINGLE PER PERSON B&B	DOUBLE FOR 2 PERSONS B&B	🛏 7 / 🛁 3
MIN £	MAX £	MIN £	MAX £	OPEN
15.00	18.50	29.00	36.00	1-12

GH | Ael y Bryn

Caernarfon Road,
Beddgelert
LL55 4UY
Tel: (01766) 890310

Mid 19th century detached house, quiet location, 5 minutes stroll to village centre. Beautiful views from our sunny terrace/garden of the River Colwyn and Moel Hebog Mountain. An ideal base for walking holidays in Snowdonia. Rooms have tea/coffee making facilities, 2 being en-suite. We offer good home cooked evening meals, including vegetarian. Parking is available.

		SINGLE PER PERSON B&B	DOUBLE FOR 2 PERSONS B&B	🛏 3 / 🛁 2
MIN £	MAX £	MIN £	MAX £	OPEN
-	-	30.00	35.00	1-12

GH | Aberconwy House

Llanrwst Road,
Betws-y-Coed
LL24 0HD
Tel: (01690) 710202
Fax: (01690) 710800

 HIGHLY COMMENDED

Aberconwy House is situated in a quiet position overlooking the popular and picturesque village. It is superbly and tastefully refurnished with all facilities for comfort and relaxation. There are beautiful views of the Llugwy Valley, surrounding mountains and the Conwy and Llugwy rivers. Robust breakfast and warm welcome awaiting from Ann and Clive Muskus.

		SINGLE PER PERSON B&B	DOUBLE FOR 2 PERSONS B&B	🛏 8 / 🛁 8
MIN £	MAX £	MIN £	MAX £	OPEN
-	-	40.00	-	1-12

GH | Coed-y-Fron

Vicarage Road,
Betws-y-Coed
LL24 0AD
Tel: (01690) 710365

A lovely Victorian building in middle of village in quiet elevated position. Superb outlook over Betws-y-Coed, which is the premier touring centre for Snowdonia. Dining room, lounge, 7 bedrooms, 2 en-suite, plus 2 extra bathrooms. All have hot and cold water, central heating, tea and coffee, colour TV. Parking. Fire certificate held. Warm welcome awaits you.

		SINGLE PER PERSON B&B	DOUBLE FOR 2 PERSONS B&B	🛏 7 / 🛁 2
MIN £	MAX £	MIN £	MAX £	OPEN
16.00	18.00	32.00	36.00	1-12

H | Princes Arms Hotel

Near Betws-y-Coed,
Trefriw
LL27 0JP
Tel: (01492) 640592
Fax: (01492) 640559

Quiet National Park location, central to Snowdonia's mountains and coast. Superb en-suite rooms with satellite TV, telephone, hairdryer, tea and coffee. Spectacular views across the River Conwy and valley. Enviable reputation for restaurant and bar meals with friendly attentive service. Open log fires. Relaxed informal atmosphere. A rather nice place to find.

		SINGLE PER PERSON B&B	DOUBLE FOR 2 PERSONS B&B	🛏 15 / 🛁 15
MIN £	MAX £	MIN £	MAX £	OPEN
20.00	20.00	40.00	40.00	1-12

GH | Bron Celyn Guest House

Llanrwst Road,
Betws-y-Coed
LL24 0HD
Tel: (01690) 710333
Fax: (01690) 710333

 HIGHLY COMMENDED

Enjoy traditional comfort and home cooked food in a relaxed atmosphere. Situated within Snowdonia National Park overlooking picturesque village of Betws-y-Coed. We provide the ideal base for walking, touring, exploring this interesting area. All rooms have colour TV, radio and beverage trays. Most en-suite. Hearty breakfasts, packed lunches, snacks, evening meals. Special diets by arrangement.

		SINGLE PER PERSON B&B	DOUBLE FOR 2 PERSONS B&B	🛏 5 / 🛁 3
MIN £	MAX £	MIN £	MAX £	OPEN
16.00	20.00	36.00	40.00	1-12

GH | Eirianfa Guest House

15-16 Castle Road,
Dolwyddelan
LL25 0NX
Tel: (01690) 750360
Fax: (01690) 750360

Homely guest house in Snowdonia Park between Betws-y-Coed and Blaenau Ffestiniog. Relaxing guest lounge. Double or twin bedded rooms. All en-suite, remote controlled colour satellite TV, tea/coffee making facilities. Excellent home cooked meals, laundry/drying service. Central for touring Snowdonia, coastal resorts, slate mines. Ideal for trekking, hiking, climbing, fishing. Reductions: short breaks, weekly stay. Brochure awaiting.

		SINGLE PER PERSON B&B	DOUBLE FOR 2 PERSONS B&B	🛏 3 / 🛁 3
MIN £	MAX £	MIN £	MAX £	OPEN
-	-	24.00	28.00	1-12

Betws-y-Coed Blaenau Ffestiniog

GH | Fron Heulog Country House

Betws-y-Coed
LL24 0BL
Tel: (01690) 710736

HIGHLY COMMENDED
AWARD

"The country house in the village!". Friendly welcome from Jean and Peter Whittingham to their elegant Victorian stone house in peaceful wooded riverside scenery, near Pont y Pair. Snowdonia's ideal centre - tour, walk, relax. Excellent modern accommodation - comfort, warmth, style. Premium bedrooms have full en-suite bathrooms. "More home than hotel!". Croeso! Welcome! *i*

P ✕ 🍴		SINGLE PER PERSON B&B	DOUBLE FOR 2 PERSONS B&B	🛏 5 🛏 5
		MIN £ 20.00	MAX £ -	MIN £ 32.00	MAX £ 40.00	OPEN 1-12

GH | Riverside Restaurant & Guest House

Holyhead Road,
Betws-y-Coed
LL24 0BN
Tel: (01690) 710650
Fax: (01690) 710650

Ⓛ

Family run restaurant and guest house offering exceptional value for money accommodation. All rooms are clean and comfortable with televisions and beverage facilities. Easy access by bus, rail and road. Our restaurant offers the best in Welsh cuisine and is featured in Taste of Wales magazine. Credit cards accepted. *i*

🍷 ✕ 🍴		SINGLE PER PERSON B&B	DOUBLE FOR 2 PERSONS B&B	🛏 4 🛏 1
		MIN £ 12.00	MAX £ 18.00	MIN £ 20.00	MAX £ 28.00	OPEN 1-12

FH | Maes y Garnedd

Capel Garmon,
Llanrwst
LL26 0RR
Tel: (01690) 710428

APPROVED
Ⓛ

A 140 acre mixed farm situated in Capel Garmon (2 miles off A5). Beautiful scenery and excellent walks. An ideal centre for touring Snowdonia and within easy reach of beaches. One double and one family bedroom. Children welcome. A warm and friendly welcome awaits you. Washbasins in bedrooms. Evening meals optional. AA Listed. SAE for brochure. *i*

P 🍴	SINGLE PER PERSON B&B	DOUBLE FOR 2 PERSONS B&B	🛏 2 🛏 1
	MIN £ 14.00	MAX £ 18.00	MIN £ 25.00	MAX £ 28.00	OPEN 1-12

GH | Glan Llugwy

Holyhead Road,
Betws-y-Coed
LL24 0BN
Tel: (01690) 710592

COMMENDED

Small friendly guest house overlooking River Llugwy and Gwyndyr Forest. Beautiful walking country all around. Central for Snowdonia mountains and coast. All rooms have central heating, hot and cold water, tea/coffee making facilities, colour TV. Guests' lounge. Private parking. Fire certificate held. Family/double twin rooms available. Showers. A warm welcome awaits you. *i*

P ✕	SINGLE PER PERSON B&B	DOUBLE FOR 2 PERSONS B&B	🛏 5 🛏 -
	MIN £ 14.00	MAX £ 16.00	MIN £ 25.00	MAX £ 28.00	OPEN 1-12

GH | Tan-y-Cyrau

Betws-y-Coed
LL24 0BL
Tel: (01690) 710653

HIGHLY COMMENDED

Peace and quiet and glorious views are what to expect at Tan-y-Cyrau. An elevated unique alpine style house situated on a private forestry road, only 5 minutes from village. Superb walks from house. Delightful rooms, two have own WC's. All have colour TV, heating, wash basins, tea/coffee making facilities. Lovely secluded gardens. Non smokers only. Good parking. *i*

P ✕ 🍴	SINGLE PER PERSON B&B	DOUBLE FOR 2 PERSONS B&B	🛏 3 🛏 2
	MIN £ -	MAX £ -	MIN £ 28.00	MAX £ 33.00	OPEN 1-12

FH | Ty Coch Farm & Trekking Centre

Penmachno,
Betws-y-Coed
LL25 0HJ
Tel: (01690) 760248

AWARD

Set in lovely valley in hills, six miles Betws-y-Coed. Excellent base for touring Snowdonia, railways, slate mines, castles and golf. Pony trekking available but optional. Comfortable accommodation and friendly personal attention. Many recommendations and return visits. Centrally heated. En-suite, TV, guests' lounge with TV and video. SAE please or ring for details any time. *i*

P 🐕 🍴 ✕	SINGLE PER PERSON B&B	DOUBLE FOR 2 PERSONS B&B	🛏 3 🛏 3
	MIN £ 16.00	MAX £ 18.00	MIN £ 32.00	MAX £ 36.00	OPEN 1-12

GH | Mount Pleasant

Holyhead Road,
Betws-y-Coed
LL24 0BN
Tel: (01690) 710502

Ⓛ

A warm Welsh welcome awaits you at our Victorian stone built house, a few minutes walk from the centre of Betws-y-Coed. Comfortable rooms all provide tea/coffee facilities, colour TV, and all have woodland views. Excellent breakfast. Vegetarian diets catered for. Walkers welcome. Packed lunches available. Children over 12 welcome. Totally non-smoking. *i*

P ✕	SINGLE PER PERSON B&B	DOUBLE FOR 2 PERSONS B&B	🛏 5 🛏 1
	MIN £ 14.00	MAX £ 18.00	MIN £ 28.00	MAX £ 38.00	OPEN 1-12

FH | Fferm Maes Gwyn

Maes Gwyn,
Pentrefoelas,
Betws-y-Coed LL24 0LR
Tel: (01690) 770668

HIGHLY COMMENDED
Ⓛ

Maes Gwyn is a 17th century farmhouse with oak beams and panelling. Separate lounge and dining room, both with log or coal fires. Situated in quiet countryside. Six miles from Betws-y-Coed, within easy reach of coast, Snowdonia, slate mines, woollen mills and much more. One double and one family room, both with tea/coffee and hot and cold water. *i*

P 🐕 Ⓒ	SINGLE PER PERSON B&B	DOUBLE FOR 2 PERSONS B&B	🛏 2 🛏 1
	MIN £ 13.50	MAX £ 14.50	MIN £ 27.00	MAX £ 29.00	OPEN 4-11

GH | Afallon

Manod Road,
Blaenau Ffestiniog
LL41 4AE
Tel: (01766) 830468

HIGHLY COMMENDED

Family run guest house situated in Snowdonia National Park. Good food, clean homely accommodation. Washbasins, shaver point, colour TV, tea/coffee facilities, central heating in all rooms. Separate shower, bathroom, toilet. Slate mines, narrow gauge railway, beaches within easy reach. Dinner by arrangement. Children reduced rates. A Welsh welcome awaits all our guests by Mrs Griffiths. *i*

P 🐕 Ⓒ ✕ 🍴	SINGLE PER PERSON B&B	DOUBLE FOR 2 PERSONS B&B	🛏 3 🛏 -
	MIN £ 12.50	MAX £ 14.50	MIN £ 25.00	MAX £ 28.00	OPEN 1-12

GH | Gwynfryn Guest House

Gellilydan
Blaenau Ffestiniog
LL41 4EA
Tel: (01766) 590225

Situated in Snowdonia National Park. Friendly welcome assured. Family run guest house in quiet area between Ffestiniog and Porthmadog, off A470 in village of Gellilydan. Slate mines, Ffestiniog Railway, castles, walks. beaches within easy reach. Many recommendations and return visits. All bedrooms with washbasins, shaver point, tea/coffee facilities, central heating. TV guest lounge. Good food. Homely welcome. *i*

		SINGLE PER PERSON B&B		DOUBLE FOR 2 PERSONS B&B		🛏 2 🛁 -
P	C	MIN £	MAX £	MIN £	MAX £	OPEN
		12.50	14.00	26.00	28.00	1-11

H | Menai Bank Hotel

North Road,
Caernarfon LL55 1BD
Tel: (01286) 673297
Fax: (01286) 673297

HIGHLY COMMENDED

Family owned period hotel, original features. Extensive sea views. Close to castle and Snowdonia. Tastefully decorated, comfortable bedrooms, one ground floor. Colour televisions, tea makers, clock radios. Attractive restaurant, varied menu, bar, residents' lounge, pool table car park, payphone. Free castles pass. Credit cards. En-suite supplement mid/high season. AA/RAC **. Colour brochure. *i*

	SINGLE PER PERSON B&B		DOUBLE FOR 2 PERSONS B&B		🛏 15 🛁 11
P	MIN £	MAX £	MIN £	MAX £	OPEN
	20.00	-	30.00	40.00	1-11

GH | Tal Menai Guest House

Bangor Road,
Caernarfon
LL55 1TP
Tel: (01286) 672160

On the outskirts of Caernarfon, Victorian guest house in its own grounds with extensive views over the Menai Strait and Anglesey. Private car park and use of garage on request, tea/coffee making facilities and radio in all rooms, TV available in rooms. Non smoking throughout, special diets catered for, French spoken. *i*

	SINGLE PER PERSON B&B		DOUBLE FOR 2 PERSONS B&B		🛏 5 🛁 1
P	MIN £	MAX £	MIN £	MAX £	OPEN
	15.00	16.00	30.00	32.00	3-10

GH | Hillcrest Guest House

Bala Road,
Ffestiniog
LL41 4PW
Tel: (01766) 762787
Fax: (01766) 762787

HIGHLY COMMENDED
L

Family home situated in the heart of Snowdonia National Park, with superb mountain views from all rooms. An area of outstanding beauty, ideal for walking, mountain activities, trekking, and the famous Ffestiniog Railway. With comfortable rooms and guests' lounge. A warm welcome awaits you, throughout the year. *i*

		SINGLE PER PERSON B&B		DOUBLE FOR 2 PERSONS B&B		🛏 3 🛁 -
P		MIN £	MAX £	MIN £	MAX £	OPEN
		15.00	15.00	30.00	30.00	1-12

GH | The Menai View Hotel

North Road,
Caernarfon
LL55 1BD
Tel: (01286) 674602

APPROVED

Victorian town house overlooking Menai Straits close to town centre and castle. Good base for mountains, lakes and railways of Snowdon. Beaches of Anglesey nearby. Also good centre for angling, riding, golf and climbing. Some sea view rooms. On main road from Bangor approaching town centre. Many local attractions. Open all year.

	SINGLE PER PERSON B&B		DOUBLE FOR 2 PERSONS B&B		🛏 8 🛁 4
C	MIN £	MAX £	MIN £	MAX £	OPEN
	16.00	19.00	25.00	33.00	1-12

GH | Tyn Llwyn Cottage

Llanllynfni,
Caernarfon,
LL54 6RP
Tel: (01286) 881526

Situated on a quiet country road, half a mile off the A487 Caernarfon to Porthmadog road, beautiful Welsh stone cottage with exposed beams and attractive garden, ideal for walking, castles, beach, birdwatching. We have two en-suite bedrooms, one on ground floor, one bedroom with private bathroom, all with colour TV. Tea/coffee made when requested. *i*

		SINGLE PER PERSON B&B		DOUBLE FOR 2 PERSONS B&B		🛏 3 🛁 2
P		MIN £	MAX £	MIN £	MAX £	OPEN
		-	-	37.00	38.00	3-10

H | Bryn Eisteddfod Hotel

Clynnog Fawr,
Caernarfon
LL54 5DA
Tel: (01286) 660431

HIGHLY COMMENDED

Situated 10 miles south of Caernarfon (A499) on outskirts of Clynnog Fawr. En-suite rooms. Colour TV, tea/coffee facilities. All rooms afford sea or mountain views. Quiet location with 1 acre garden. Vegetarian meals available, real ale. Children welcome. 2 night D, B&B breaks from £46pp, single room supplement £5pp pn. Sorry no dogs. Excellent restaurant situated in large Victorian style conservatory. *i*

		SINGLE PER PERSON B&B		DOUBLE FOR 2 PERSONS B&B		🛏 10 🛁 8
P		MIN £	MAX £	MIN £	MAX £	OPEN
		-	-	34.00	40.00	1-12

GH | Hen Ysgol (Old School)

Bwlch-Derwin, Pant Glas,
Garndolbenmaen
LL51 9EQ
Tel: (01286) 660701

Old Welsh school, dated 1858, retaining character with a past in rural Wales. Centrally located for the attractions of Snowdonia and the Llŷn Peninsula. Midway between Caernarfon and Porthmadog, off A487. Ground floor rooms providing ease of access, including en-suite family room. Ample off road parking, evening meals available on request. Bring your own wine! *i*

		SINGLE PER PERSON B&B		DOUBLE FOR 2 PERSONS B&B		🛏 3 🛁 1
P		MIN £	MAX £	MIN £	MAX £	OPEN
		14.50	17.50	29.00	35.00	1-12

GH | The White House

Llanfaglan,
Caernarfon
LL54 5RA
Tel: (01286) 673003

HIGHLY COMMENDED

Large quietly situated country house in own grounds with magnificent views to sea and mountains. All rooms have en-suite or private facilities, colour TV, tea/coffee makers. One bedroom on ground floor. Guests are welcome to use lounge, outdoor pool in summer, and gardens. Ideally situated for ornithologists, walkers, golf, and visiting castles and the National Park. *i*

		SINGLE PER PERSON B&B		DOUBLE FOR 2 PERSONS B&B		🛏 4 🛁 3
P		MIN £	MAX £	MIN £	MAX £	OPEN
C		19.00	20.00	34.00	38.00	3-11

Caernarfon   Capel Curig   Conwy   Corris   Corwen   Criccieth

---

FH   Pengwern

Saron, Llanwnda,
Caernarfon LL54 5UH
Tel: (01286) 831500
Mobile: (0378) 411780
Fax: (01286) 831500

Charming spacious farmhouse of character set in 130 acres of land, beautifully situated between mountains and sea. Well appointed bedrooms, all en-suite. Our land runs down to Foryd Bay and is noted for its bird life. Situated 3 miles from Dinas Dinlle beach. Jane Rowlands has a cookery diploma and provides all the excellent meals. Some of the executive en-suites may have surcharge, please ask. *i*

P ⚑	SINGLE PER PERSON B&B		DOUBLE FOR 2 PERSONS B&B		🛏 3
⚒ 🍴					🛁 3
	MIN £	MAX £	MIN £	MAX £	OPEN
	-	-	40.00	40.00	2-11

GH   Coedlyn

Ro-wen,
Conwy
LL32 8YL
Tel: (01492) 650469

If you enjoy hill walking in peaceful and tranquil surroundings, come to Coedlyn, situated in the stress free Conwy Valley, Snowdonia National Park, between two fishing lakes, with lovely gardens, log fires and home fayre. Perfect for visiting North Wales holiday attractions, Bodnant Garden, castles, beaches, golf and horse riding. A warm welcome awaits you. Croeso. *i*

P ⚑	SINGLE PER PERSON B&B		DOUBLE FOR 2 PERSONS B&B		🛏 2
⚒ C					🛁 1
🍴	MIN £	MAX £	MIN £	MAX £	OPEN
	16.50	18.50	32.00	38.00	2-12

GH   Tyn-Llidiart House

Corwen
LL21 9RS
Tel: (01490) 412729

HIGHLY COMMENDED

A country house set in Dee Valley. By River Dee overlooking Berwyn Mountains. Corwen is an ideal base for exploring North Wales, both countryside and coast. En-suite rooms with colour TV, tea/coffee facilities. Hairdryers, shampoos and bathfoam aids. Tastefully decorated house with pleasant surroundings and a very warm welcome. *i*

C ⚒	SINGLE PER PERSON B&B		DOUBLE FOR 2 PERSONS B&B		🛏 2
✂					🛁 2
	MIN £	MAX £	MIN £	MAX £	OPEN
	16.50	16.50	33.00	33.00	1-12

GH   Bryn Glo Cafe

Bryn Glo, Capel Curig,
Near Betws-y-Coed
LL24 0DT
Tel: (01690) 720215/720312

Enjoy the splendours of Snowdonia from our family run tea room and guest house. Easy access on A5 Holyhead road. Warm welcome from Taste of Wales members, with home cooked food served all day. Tea and coffee facilities in rooms. *i*

P ⚒	SINGLE PER PERSON B&B		DOUBLE FOR 2 PERSONS B&B		🛏 6
⚒ 🍴					🛁 2
	MIN £	MAX £	MIN £	MAX £	OPEN
	16.00	17.00	28.00	30.00	1-12

GH   Glan Heulog Guest House

Woodlands,
Llanrwst Road,
Conwy LL32 8LT
Tel: (01492) 593845

Close to Conwy Castle and historic old town. An ideal centre for touring Snowdonia, North Wales coast, Bodnant Garden. Colour TV, tea/coffee in all bedrooms. Our guests say, "wonderful meals", "great rooms", "excellent service", "charming hosts", "lovely warm welcome", "best place I've stayed", "we will be back". Quiet location. Good views. *i*

P ⚑	SINGLE PER PERSON B&B		DOUBLE FOR 2 PERSONS B&B		🛏 7
⚒ ✂					🛁 4
🍴	MIN £	MAX £	MIN £	MAX £	OPEN
	13.00	18.00	26.00	32.00	1-12

H   Glyn y Coed Hotel

Porthmadog Road,
Criccieth LL52 0HP
Tel: (01766) 522870
Fax: (01766) 523341

HIGHLY COMMENDED

Lovely Victorian house overlooking sea, mountains and castles. Cosy bar. Highly recommended. Home cooking catering for most diets. En-suite bedrooms (one ground floor), colour TV's, tea making facilities, private parking. Special children and senior rates. AA/RAC Acclaimed, Les Routiers. Credit card accepted. Also self-catering bungalow, sleeps 8. Brochure with pleasure, SAE please. *i*

P ⚑	SINGLE PER PERSON B&B		DOUBLE FOR 2 PERSONS B&B		🛏 10
C ⚑					🛁 10
⚒ ✂ 🍴	MIN £	MAX £	MIN £	MAX £	OPEN
	20.00	-	20.00	-	1-12

GH   Llugwy Guest House

Capel Curig,
Near Betws-y-Coed
LL24 0ES
Tel: (01690) 720218

COMMENDED

Established over 100 years, located in centre of village, five miles from Snowdon. Ideal for walking, climbing, fishing, boating, beaches, small trains, castles, ski slope. Two public lounges, one with TV, beamed dining room, central heating. Tea/coffee in bedrooms. Superb mountain views. Private car park. Friendly advice on local area, if required. *i*

P ⚑	SINGLE PER PERSON B&B		DOUBLE FOR 2 PERSONS B&B		🛏 6
⚒ ✂ 🍴					
	MIN £	MAX £	MIN £	MAX £	OPEN
	16.00	18.00	28.00	30.00	1-12

H   Braich Goch Hotel

Corris
SY20 9RD
Tel: (01654) 761229
Fax: (01654) 761229

COMMENDED

Set in beautiful surroundings at head of Dulas Valley. All rooms en-suite or private facilities. Bar meals or restaurant. The Centre for Alternative Technology, King Arthur's Labyrinth and Celtica Centre all nearby. Beach is within easy reach. Rich in mountain walks, steam trains, golf, fishing, horse riding. Activity holidays arranged. Pets welcome. Children 5 years +. *i*

P ⚑	SINGLE PER PERSON B&B		DOUBLE FOR 2 PERSONS B&B		🛏 6
⚑ ✂					🛁 6
🍴	MIN £	MAX £	MIN £	MAX £	OPEN
	-	-	35.00	39.00	1-12

H   The Lion Hotel

Y Maes,
Criccieth LL52 0AA
Tel: (01766) 522460
Fax: (01766) 523075

COMMENDED

Ideally sited for touring Snowdonia and the Llŷn Peninsula. This comfortable hotel is on the village green in the centre of the beautiful coastal town of Criccieth. It offers the visitor excellent value with every modern facility at B&B terms. Private gardens. Views of the bay and castle. Fully licensed, with weekly entertainment programmes. *i*

P ⚑	SINGLE PER PERSON B&B		DOUBLE FOR 2 PERSONS B&B		🛏 45
⚑ 🍴					🛁 45
✂	MIN £	MAX £	MIN £	MAX £	OPEN
	19.50	-	38.00	-	1-12

H | Min y Gaer Hotel

Porthmadog Road,
Criccieth LL52 0HP
Tel: (01766) 522151
Fax: (01766) 522151

COMMENDED

A pleasant licensed hotel, conveniently situated near the beach with delightful views of Criccieth Castle and the Cardigan Bay coastline. Ten comfortable centrally heated rooms, all with colour TV and tea/coffee making facilities. An ideal base for touring Snowdonia and the Llŷn Peninsula. Reduced rates for children. Private car parking. AA Recommended. RAC Acclaimed.

		SINGLE PER PERSON B&B		DOUBLE FOR 2 PERSONS B&B		🛏 10 / 9
		MIN £	MAX £	MIN £	MAX £	OPEN
		17.50	20.00	35.00	40.00	3-10

GH | Dwy Olwyn

Coed-y-Fronallt,
Dolgellau
LL40 2YG
Tel: (01341) 422822

COMMENDED

A comfortable guest house situated in an acre of landscaped gardens. Boasting magnificent views in a peaceful position, yet only 10 minutes' walk to the town. Close to all amenities and numerous walks. Good home cooking. Personal attention assured. Ample parking, lounge with colour TV. Tea/coffee facilities in all bedrooms.

	SINGLE PER PERSON B&B		DOUBLE FOR 2 PERSONS B&B		🛏 3
	MIN £	MAX £	MIN £	MAX £	OPEN
	-	-	26.00	-	2-12

GH | Tanyfron

Arran Road,
Dolgellau LL40 2AA
Tel: (01341) 422638
Fax: (01341) 422638

HIGHLY COMMENDED

A warm welcome awaits you in our comfortable, quiet, modernised, 100 year old former farmhouse. Lovely views. 0.5 miles from Dolgellau. Tastefully furnished with matching decor. All rooms have tea making, hairdryers, heating, clock radio and colour TV with Sky Channels. Laundry and public telephone are also available for guests' use. Parking in our own grounds. Non smokers.

		SINGLE PER PERSON B&B		DOUBLE FOR 2 PERSONS B&B		🛏 3 / 3
		MIN £	MAX £	MIN £	MAX £	OPEN
		-	-	35.00	36.00	2-11

GH | Neptune Môr Heli

Min y Mor,
Criccieth
LL52 0EF
Tel: (01766) 522802

Situated on the sea front overlooking Cardigan Bay. All rooms en-suite, TV etc. Noted for good food and friendly atmosphere. Run by Williams family for over 20 years. AA Recommended

		SINGLE PER PERSON B&B		DOUBLE FOR 2 PERSONS B&B		🛏 8 / 8
		MIN £	MAX £	MIN £	MAX £	OPEN
		16.00	20.00	32.00	40.00	1-12

GH | Llety Nêst

Brithdir,
Dolgellau
LL40 2RY
Tel: (01341) 450326

HIGHLY COMMENDED

Situated 3 miles from Dolgellau in Snowdonia National Park. Bungalow on its own with 90 acres of land. Fantastic scenery, beautiful walks, 9 miles from sea and by the mountains. Friendly hosts to look after you. Two rooms: 1 family room with 1 double and 2 singles; 1 double room. Both en-suite with patchwork quilts. Separate dining room and separate lounge. Good home cooked food provided.

		SINGLE PER PERSON B&B		DOUBLE FOR 2 PERSONS B&B		🛏 2 / 2
		MIN £	MAX £	MIN £	MAX £	OPEN
		15.00	17.00	32.00	-	3-11

GH | Trem Idris

Llanelltyd,
Near Dolgellau
LL40 2TB
Tel: (01341) 423776

Trem Idris, an artist's paradise, situated in a elevated position overlooking the outstandingly beautiful Mawddach Estuary and with extensive panoramic views of Cader Idris Mountains. Most rooms en-suite, one ground floor. All rooms with colour TV, tea/coffee facilities. Renowned for scenic walks. Ideally situated for exploring Snowdonia. Homely relaxed atmosphere.

		SINGLE PER PERSON B&B		DOUBLE FOR 2 PERSONS B&B		🛏 2 / 2
		MIN £	MAX £	MIN £	MAX £	OPEN
		-	-	-	-	1-12

FH | Bryncelyn Farm

Dinas Mawddwy,
Machynlleth
SY20 9JG
Tel: (01650) 531289

A warm welcome awaits you at Bryncelyn Farm, located in the peaceful valley of Cowarch at the foot of Aran Fawddwy. An excellent centre for walking, climbing and touring. Spacious en-suite bedrooms with tea/coffee making facilities, colour television and heating. Ideal base for touring Mid Wales, Snowdonia and seaside resorts. Five minutes away from main north to south road, A470.

		SINGLE PER PERSON B&B		DOUBLE FOR 2 PERSONS B&B		🛏 2 / 2
		MIN £	MAX £	MIN £	MAX £	OPEN
		16.00	18.00	32.00	36.00	1-12

GH | Llwyn Talcen

Brithdir,
Dolgellau
LL40 2RY
Tel: (01341) 450276

L

Situated in large rhododendron and azalea gardens, Llwyn Talcen offers a warm welcome. Outstanding views together with peace and quiet. Ideal centre for hill walkers, nature lovers and touring. We offer delicious meals. Vegetarians catered for. Children welcome. 0.5 miles from village phone box, off lane to Bryncoedifor, turn right before campsite. House second right.

		SINGLE PER PERSON B&B		DOUBLE FOR 2 PERSONS B&B		🛏 3 / 1
		MIN £	MAX £	MIN £	MAX £	OPEN
		15.00	18.00	30.00	36.00	1-12

GH | Y Goedlan

Brithdir,
Dolgellau
LL40 2RN
Tel: (01341) 423131

This old vicarage offers peaceful accommodation in pleasant rural surroundings. Ideally placed on B4416 road for walks, sea, mountains and touring. Spacious double, twin and family rooms. All with H&C, colour TV, central heating, tea/coffee facilities. Bathroom with shower, two conveniences and lounge. Comfort with homely atmosphere. Hearty breakfast. Reduction for children. Dolgellau 2 miles.

		SINGLE PER PERSON B&B		DOUBLE FOR 2 PERSONS B&B		🛏 3
		MIN £	MAX £	MIN £	MAX £	OPEN
		16.50	-	28.00	30.00	2-11

Dolgellau   Fairbourne   Harlech   Llanbedr-y-Cennin   Llanberis

---

FH | Arosfyr Farm

Penycefn Road,
Dolgellau
LL40 2YP
Tel: (01341) 422355

Arosfyr on the way to Dolgellau golf course, has panoramic views of Cader Idris Mountains. Ideal for touring, walking, climbing, pony trekking, narrow gauge railways, castles, gold and slate mines. Double, family and twin bedrooms with heating, wash basins. Dining room, lounge, tea/coffee making facilities, TV. Friendly welcome, relaxed atmosphere, access all times, parking. Flower gardens a speciality. Good hearty breakfast with own free range eggs. i

		SINGLE PER PERSON B&B		DOUBLE FOR 2 PERSONS B&B		🛏 3 🛁
P	🛏	MIN £ 15.00	MAX £ -	MIN £ 27.00	MAX £ -	OPEN 1-12

GH | Einion House

Friog,
Fairbourne
LL38 2NX
Tel: (01341) 250644

COMMENDED

Lovely old house set in beautiful scenery between mountains and sea. Reputation for good home cooking. Vegetarians catered for. All rooms colour TV, clock radio, hairdryer, tea maker. Marvellous walking, maps available. Pony trekking, fishing and birdwatching. Good centre for narrow gauge railways. Castles easy reach. Safe sandy beach few minutes' walk from house. i

		SINGLE PER PERSON B&B		DOUBLE FOR 2 PERSONS B&B		🛏 7 🛁 5
🐕 ♟	🍴	MIN £ 19.00	MAX £ 19.00	MIN £ 32.00	MAX £ 35.00	OPEN 1-12

FH | Gwrach Ynys Country Guest House

Ynys,
Talsarnau
LL47 6TS
Tel: (01766) 780742
Fax: (01766) 781199

DE LUXE

Treat yourself to a refreshing peaceful break in the glorious, rural setting of our country guest house. Friendly welcome and imaginative home cooking. Bedrooms en-suite with colour TV's and beverage facilities. Close to sea, mountains, swimming pool, golf and lovely estuary walks. Many interesting local attractions. Illustrated brochure sent with pleasure. Croeso Cymreig. i

		SINGLE PER PERSON B&B		DOUBLE FOR 2 PERSONS B&B		🛏 7 🛁 6
P 🛏	C 🍴	MIN £ 17.50	MAX £ 20.00	MIN £ 35.00	MAX £ 40.00	OPEN 1-12

FH | Gwanas Farmhouse

Cross Foxes,
Dolgellau LL40 2SH
Tel: (01341) 422624
Fax: (01341) 422624

Charming spacious farmhouse built in 1838. Peaceful setting. Tom and Mair Evans farm sheep and cattle on 1,000 acres. Twin, double or family rooms with H&C, two bathrooms with showers. Central heating, tea/coffee facilities in bedrooms. Delicious breakfast. TV, Ideal touring base. Situated 400 yards from Cross Foxes Inn, off A470, three miles from Dolgellau. i

		SINGLE PER PERSON B&B		DOUBLE FOR 2 PERSONS B&B		🛏 3 🛁 -
P	MIN £ 16.00	MAX £ 18.00	MIN £ 28.00	MAX £ 30.00		OPEN 3-10

GH | Glanygors Guest House

Llandanwg,
Harlech
LL46 2SD
Tel: (01341) 241410

Small friendly guest house in own grounds. Situated 400 yards from sandy beach. All rooms have washbasin, TV, tea and coffee making facilities, electric blanket and central heating. Beautiful views from all windows. Private access to beach. Near train station. Ample parking. Golf, rambling, birdwatching, sailing, fishing - all to be found in the area. Warm Welsh welcome i

		SINGLE PER PERSON B&B		DOUBLE FOR 2 PERSONS B&B		🛏 3 🛁 -
P	🍴	MIN £ 13.50	MAX £ -	MIN £ 26.00	MAX £ 28.00	OPEN 1-12

GH | Church House

Llanbedr-y-Cennin,
Conwy Valley
LL32 8JB
Tel: (01492) 660521

HIGHLY COMMENDED

Lovely 16th century listed building with oak beams and inglenook fireplaces. Central heating, TV, hot and cold water and tea trays in its two double bedrooms. Situated in a small village, coupled with 16th century inn, in the Snowdonia foothills, just off the B5106, between Conwy and Betws-y-Coed. Ideal for sightseeing, walking, coast etc. i

		SINGLE PER PERSON B&B		DOUBLE FOR 2 PERSONS B&B		🛏 2 🛁 -
P	🐕 🍴	MIN £ -	MAX £ 19.50	MIN £ -	MAX £ 34.00	OPEN 1-12

FH | Tyddynmawr Farmhouse

Islawrdref,
Dolgellau
LL40 1TL
Tel: (01341) 422331

DE LUXE

It's paradise! Honestly! A warm welcome awaits you in this lovingly restored 18th century farmhouse. Beams, log fires. All bedrooms en-suite, with superb mountain views. We farm the magnificent mountain of Cader Idris and have waterfalls, slate mines, caves and fishing on mountain lake on farm. We offer peace, tranquillity and seclusion. i

		SINGLE PER PERSON B&B		DOUBLE FOR 2 PERSONS B&B		🛏 2 🛁 2
P	MIN £ -	MAX £ -	MIN £ -	MAX £ 40.00		OPEN 4-11

GH | Godre 'r Graig

Ffordd Newydd,
Lower Harlech
LL46 2UD
Tel: (01766) 780905

COMMENDED

Warm friendly welcome guaranteed. Nestling below Harlech Castle, within sight of Royal St David's Golf Club. Children's rates, occasional babysitting. TV lounge. Home cooked evening meals by arrangement with great vegetarian choice. Vanity units, hot drinks tray. The beautiful Snowdonia National Park, wonderful beaches, pony trekking, trout and sea fishing. Fantasy ceramic packages. i

		SINGLE PER PERSON B&B		DOUBLE FOR 2 PERSONS B&B		🛏 4 🛁 -
P	🍴	MIN £ 17.00	MAX £ -	MIN £ 29.00	MAX £ -	OPEN 1-12

H | Gwynedd Hotel

High Street,
Llanberis LL55 4SU
Tel: (01286) 870203
Fax: (01286) 871636

HIGHLY COMMENDED

Set at the foot of Snowdon and opposite Lake Padarn with its magnificent surroundings, the Gwynedd is an ideal touring and walking base. There are eleven fully equipped en-suite guest rooms. The lounge bar provide a relaxing setting to enjoy a drink or bar meal, alternatively the elegant restaurant provides a comprehensive à la carte menu. i

		SINGLE PER PERSON B&B		DOUBLE FOR 2 PERSONS B&B		🛏 11 🛁 -
🐕	🍴	MIN £ 18.00	MAX £ 20.00	MIN £ 36.00	MAX £ 40.00	OPEN 1-12

GH | Bron y Graig

Capel Coch Road,
Llanberis
LL55 4SH
Tel: (01286) 872073

Picturesque Llanberis, in the heart of the Snowdonia National Park, provides an excellent base for walking, climbing or sightseeing holidays. Anglesey's beautiful beaches are nearby. Bron y Graig is a family run house with spacious gardens in a quiet location close to the village centre. Rooms are furnished to a high standard, including en-suite. *i*

SINGLE PER PERSON B&B		DOUBLE FOR 2 PERSONS B&B		🛏 2 🛁 1
MIN £	MAX £	MIN £	MAX £	OPEN
13.00	16.00	30.00	38.00	1-12

GH | Maenllwyd

Newtown Road,
Machynlleth SY20 8EY
Tel: (01654) 702928
Fax: (01654) 702928

HIGHLY COMMENDED AWARD

Friendly guest house in historic market town. All rooms en-suite, centrally heated, tea/coffee making facilities, TV. We are noted for our breakfasts. Secure off road parking. Lounge with books, video's. Convenient for golf, hill walking, bird watching, leisure centre, beaches, Centre for Alternative Technology. For further information telephone Nigel or Margaret Vince. *i*

SINGLE PER PERSON B&B		DOUBLE FOR 2 PERSONS B&B		🛏 8 🛁 8
MIN £	MAX £	MIN £	MAX £	OPEN
20.00	25.00	35.00	37.00	1-12

GH | Min-y-Ddol

Minffordd,
Penrhyndeudraeth
LL48 6HL
Tel: (01766) 771458

Located one mile from Porthmadog, and within easy walking distance of Portmeirion, enjoying magnificent views. Perfect centre for walking, sightseeing and sandy beaches. Modern accommodation with all facilities. *i*

SINGLE PER PERSON B&B		DOUBLE FOR 2 PERSONS B&B		🛏 3 🛁 1
MIN £	MAX £	MIN £	MAX £	OPEN
-	-	28.00	33.00	1-12

GH | Crochendy Guest House

Mur Mawr,
Llanberis,
Near Caernarfon LL55 4TG
Tel: (01286) 870700

Small guest house with excellent facilities in secluded setting within Snowdonia National Park. Delightful garden overlooking Padarn Lake and Llanberis village. Easy access to many places of interest and recreational activities. Personal service from proprietors Jane and Peter Richards. Food is excellent and plentiful. Special diets are catered for. Packed lunches available on request. *i*

SINGLE PER PERSON B&B		DOUBLE FOR 2 PERSONS B&B		🛏 3 🛁 1
MIN £	MAX £	MIN £	MAX £	OPEN
-	-	25.00	36.00	2-11

GH | Pendre Guest House

Maengwyn Street,
Machynlleth
SY20 8EF
Tel: (01654) 702088

COMMENDED

Welcome to our friendly home Pendre is a Georgian house with large rooms in the centre of Machynlleth town. Close to railway station, Centre for Alternative Technology, Celtica, sports centre walking, fishing and beautiful coastline and beaches. All rooms have colour TV. Off road parking. Contact Elaine Petrie. *i*

SINGLE PER PERSON B&B		DOUBLE FOR 2 PERSONS B&B		🛏 3 🛁 2
MIN £	MAX £	MIN £	MAX £	OPEN
18.00	20.00	31.00	35.00	1-12

GH | The Oakleys Guest House

The Harbour,
Porthmadog
LL49 9AS
Tel: (01766) 512482

L

Situated on the harbour in Porthmadog. An excellent base for visiting Snowdonia, Portmeirion and the beaches of the Llŷn Peninsula taking in Pwllheli, Abersoch and Criccieth. Fishing - sea trout/salmon, golf course nearby. Spacious free car park. Comfortable lounge, informal holiday atmosphere, 2 bedrooms with showers, one en-suite bedroom. Electric blankets. Contact Mr & Mrs H. A. Biddle.

SINGLE PER PERSON B&B		DOUBLE FOR 2 PERSONS B&B		🛏 8 🛁 3
MIN £	MAX £	MIN £	MAX £	OPEN
14.00	16.00	28.00	30.00	3-10

GH | The White Cottage

Maenan (A470),
Llanrwst
LL26 0UL
Tel: (01492) 640346

Situated in the beautiful Conwy Valley, 2 miles north of Llanrwst. All rooms have scenic views, hot and cold water, central heating. Bathroom with shower and separate toilet. Comfortable lounge with colour TV. Relax in lovely garden or stroll in woodland dells. Two hotels close for evening meals. Bodnant Garden and many local attractions within easy reach. *i*

SINGLE PER PERSON B&B		DOUBLE FOR 2 PERSONS B&B		🛏 3 🛁 -
MIN £	MAX £	MIN £	MAX £	OPEN
16.00	16.00	30.00	30.00	1-12

FH | Mathafarn

Llanwrin,
Machynlleth
SY20 8QJ
Tel: (01650) 511226

HIGHLY COMMENDED

Henry VII is reputed to have stayed here en-route to the Battle of Bosworth. Now this 16th century elegant country house is part of a working farm. Inglenook fire, central heating, television lounge, one twin, private bathroom, double en-suite. Tea/coffee making facilities. Close to Machynlleth, Centre for Alternative Technology, beautiful coastline of Aberdyfi. Contact Susan Hughes. *i*

SINGLE PER PERSON B&B		DOUBLE FOR 2 PERSONS B&B		🛏 2 🛁 1
MIN £	MAX £	MIN £	MAX £	OPEN
17.00	17.00	34.00	35.00	1-12

GH | Skellerns

35 Madoc Street,
Porthmadog
LL49 9BU
Tel: (01766) 512843

Friendly welcome for all. Good home cooking, heating in all rooms. Colour TV and tea/coffee making facilities in all rooms. Keys supplied. Special rates for children. Shops, buses, trains, centre nearby. Ideally situated for visiting Portmeirion Italianate Village, the mountains of Snowdonia and the Ffestiniog Railway. Sandy beaches nearby. Open all year. Proprietor Mrs R. Skellern. *i*

SINGLE PER PERSON B&B		DOUBLE FOR 2 PERSONS B&B		🛏 3 🛁 -
MIN £	MAX £	MIN £	MAX £	OPEN
12.00	14.00	24.00	28.00	1-12

Porthmadog Tal-y-llyn Tywyn

GH	Ty-Newydd

30 Dublin Street,
Tremadog,
Porthmadog LL49 9RH
Tel: (01766) 512553

ⓛ

Family bedroom, two doubles. Private car park. Central for all parts, Ffestiniog and Snowdon Railways and beaches. Hot and cold in all rooms.

i

P	✂	SINGLE PER PERSON B&B	DOUBLE FOR 2 PERSONS B&B	🛏 3
				🛁 2

MIN £ 15.00	MAX £ -	MIN £ 14.00	MAX £ 28.00	OPEN 3-9

H	Greenfield Hotel

High Street,
Tywyn LL36 9AD
Tel: (01654) 710354
Fax: (01654) 710354

👑👑

AA*, RAC*, well established, family run hotel close to all amenities including shops, beach, BR and Talyllyn Narrow Gauge Railway. Opposite leisure centre and large car park. Evening meals available. Colour TV and beverage making facilities in all rooms. Residents' lounge, licensed bar. 5 miles from Aberdovey Golf Links. Brochure available on request, contact Cynthia Jenkins.

i

C	🍷	SINGLE PER PERSON B&B	DOUBLE FOR 2 PERSONS B&B	🛏 8
🏠	🍽			🛁 5

MIN £ 17.00	MAX £ 19.50	MIN £ 34.00	MAX £ 39.00	OPEN 1-11

GH	Pant y Neuadd Country House

Aberdovey Road,
Tywyn
LL36 9HW
Tel: (01654) 711393

👑👑

Enjoy a peaceful break within a quiet holiday environment. 15 minutes' stroll away from Tywyn along Lover Lane, enjoying magnificent views. Originally the home of Sir Hayden Jones (Talyllyn Railway), now modernised yet retaining its character, log fires, oak panelling. Three en-suite bedrooms, colour TV's and tea makers. Safe parking. A warm welcome awaits you.

i

P	🐕	SINGLE PER PERSON B&B	DOUBLE FOR 2 PERSONS B&B	🛏 3
				🛁 3

MIN £ 16.00	MAX £ 19.00	MIN £ 32.00	MAX £ 34.00	OPEN 4-9

FH	Dolffanog Fach

Tal-y-llyn,
Tywyn LL36 9AJ
Tel: (01654) 761235
Fax: (01654) 761235

 👑👑

Stone built farmhouse situated near Talyllyn Lake at the foot of Cader Idris. En-suite bedroom available, or bedrooms with wash basins, colour TV, tea/coffee making facilities. Good home cooking. Ideal touring centre. Walking, fishing, trekking, Centre for Alternative Technology or Cader Idris. Games room with full size snooker table, or relax in the garden. Contact Mrs Meirwen Pughe.

i

P	🐕	SINGLE PER PERSON B&B	DOUBLE FOR 2 PERSONS B&B	🛏 3
🏠	✂			🛁 1
🍽				

MIN £ 15.00	MAX £ 18.00	MIN £ 30.00	MAX £ 36.00	OPEN 2-11

GH	Glenfield

10 Idris Villas,
Tywyn
LL36 9AW
Tel: (01654) 710707

ⓛ

Homely accommodation near shops, railway, bus station. Ten minutes' walk from beach and five minutes' walk from swimming pool and leisure centre. Overlooking Cader Idris Mountain range. Five minutes walk from the famous Talyllyn Railway. Ideal centre for walking, fishing, sailing, and golf. Personal supervision.

i

🐕	🏠	SINGLE PER PERSON B&B	DOUBLE FOR 2 PERSONS B&B	🛏 3
✂				🛁 -

MIN £ 14.00	MAX £ 16.00	MIN £ 28.00	MAX £ 32.00	OPEN 3-10

H	Corbett Arms Hotel

Corbett Square,
Tywyn LL36 9DG
Tel: (01654) 710264
Fax: (01654) 710359

 👑👑

Delightful old inn offering superb touring location near Snowdonia National Park and Cambrian Coast. Warm and friendly welcome assured. Rooms with private bath or shower, WC, colour TV, beverage making facilities. Some four posters/waterbeds available. Restaurant serves an appetising cuisine based on local produce. 3 bars with real ale. Lift. Attractive, enclosed Victorian garden.

i

P	🐕	SINGLE PER PERSON B&B	DOUBLE FOR 2 PERSONS B&B	🛏 42
C				🛁 42
🏠	✂			
🍽				

MIN £ 12.00	MAX £ 20.00	MIN £ 24.00	MAX £ 40.00	OPEN 1-12

Tal-y-llyn

This large area encompasses the rural heartlands of Wales. From the unexplored Berwyn Mountains in the north to the grassy heights of the Brecon Beacons in the south, the predominant colour is green. And the predominant mood is restful, for this is Wales's most peaceful and unhurried area, a place of quiet country roads and small market towns, hill sheep farms and rolling borderlands. It's also a place of scenic lakes — the Elan Valley, Clywedog and Vyrnwy – set in undisturbed landscapes rich in wildlife, where you may spot the rare red kite circling in the skies. And Wales's great outdoors doesn't come any greater than in the Brecon Beacons National Park, whose wide, open spaces were made for walking and pony trekking.

It's a fact...

The Brecon Beacons National Park, covering 519 square miles, was designated in 1957. The Beacons' peak of Pen-y-fan, at 886m/2907ft, is the highest summit in South Wales. The Elan Valley reservoirs, created between 1892 and 1903, were the first of Wales's man-made lakelands. Pistyll Rhaeadr, near Llanrhaeadr ym Mochnant, is the highest waterfall in England and Wales, plunging 73m/240ft. Sections of the 8th-century earthwork known as Offa's Dyke – the first official border between England and Wales – still stand almost to their full height in the hills around Knighton.

Ge6　Brecon

Main touring centre for the 519 square miles of the Brecon Beacons National Park. Handsome old town with thriving market, ruined castle, cathedral (with its imaginative Heritage Centre), priory, two interesting museums (Brecknock and South Wales Borderers') and Welsh Whisky Experience attraction. Wide range of inns and good shopping. Centre for walking and pony trekking. Golf, fishing and canal cruising also available. Very popular summer International Jazz Festival.

Ge4　Builth Wells

Solidly built old country town which plays host every July to the Royal Welsh Agricultural Show, Wales's largest farming gathering. Lovely setting on River Wye amid beautiful hills. Lively sheep and cattle markets. Good shopping for local products, touring centre for Mid Wales and border country. River walk, Wyeside Arts Centre.

Hb7　Crickhowell

Small, pleasant country town beautifully situated on the River Usk. Good for walking, fishing, pony trekking and riding. Remains of Norman castle, 14th-century Tretower Court and earlier castle worth a visit.

Ha5　Erwood

Small village on banks of the River Wye south-east of Builth Wells. Good base for fishing and walking – village is close to Brecon Beacons National Park, hills of central Wales and rolling border country.

Ha6　Felinfach

Village in rolling border setting between Brecon and Hay-on-Wye. Handy for exploring the Brecon Beacons, Wye and Usk valleys, and the hills of Mid Wales. Excellent walking, fishing and pony trekking countryside. Llangorse Lake, South Wales's largest lake, nearby.

Hb5　Hay-on-Wye

Small market town on the Offa's Dyke Path, nestling beneath the Black Mountains on a picturesque stretch of the River Wye. A mecca for book lovers – there are antiquarian and second-hand bookshops, some huge, all over the town. Attractive crafts centre. Literature Festival in early summer attracts big names.

Ge3　Llandrindod Wells　

Victorian spa town with spacious streets and impressive architecture. Victorian-style visitor centre and excellent museum tracing the history of spa. Magic Lantern Theatre. A popular inland resort with golf, fishing, bowling, boating and tennis available. Excellent touring centre for Mid Wales hills and lakes. Annual Victorian Festival in August.

Eb5　Llanfair Caereinion

Pleasant town set amid rolling hills and forests in lovely Vale of Banwy. Best known as the terminus for narrow-gauge Welshpool and Llanfair Light Railway.

Gc1　Llangurig

First village on fledgling River Wye, around 300m/1000ft up in the mountains. A craft centre and a monastic 14th-century church. Good touring centre for lakes and mountains of central Wales. Ideal walking countryside.

Craig-goch dam, Elan Valley

48

Gd1   Llanidloes

Historic and attractive market town at confluence of Severn and Clywedog rivers; excellent touring centre. Noted for its 16th-century market hall, now a museum, and other fine half-timbered buildings. Interesting shops. Massive Clywedog dam and lake 3 miles away on B4518. Take the scenic drive around lakeside and visit the Bryn Tail Lead Mine beneath the dam.

Ea3   Llanwddyn

Village the foot of dramatic, mountain-ringed Lake Vyrnwy. Ideal for peaceful country holidays – walking, fishing, birdwatching. Vyrnwy Visitor Centre has information on the lake and the rich wildlife of the surrounding forests, hills and mountains.

Gc5   Llanwrtyd Wells

One-time spa encircled by wild and beautiful countryside, now a centre for pony trekking, walking, fishing and mountain biking. Cambrian Woollen Mill a popular attraction. For spectacular views explore nearby Abergwesyn Pass/Llyn Brianne area. Diverse programme of events throughout the year.

Ec6   Montgomery

Hilltop market town of distinctive Georgian architecture beneath the ruins of a 13th-century castle. Offa's Dyke, which once marked the border, runs nearby. Not far from Welshpool and Powis Castle.

Eb6   Newtown

Busy Severn Valley market town and one-time home of Welsh flannel industry. Textile history recalled in small museum; another museum based around Robert Owen, pioneer socialist, who lived here. Town also has interesting W H Smith Museum, solid old buildings, river promenade, street market and the lively Theatr Hafren.

Eb3   Penybontfawr

Secluded village amid forest and lake, near the spectacular 73m/240ft Pistyll Rhaeadr waterfall. Pony trekking and walking country, with hills and woods all around. Lake Vyrnwy Visitor Centre nearby.

Hc2   Presteigne

Typical black-and-white half-timbered border town with ancient inns; the Radnorshire Arms has secret passages. Pony trekking available – the perfect way to explore this tranquil wooded countryside. Offa's Dyke Path nearby.

Gd2   Rhayader

Country market town full of character, with inviting inns and Welsh craft products in the shops. Excellent base for exploring mountains and lakes (Elan Valley and Claerwen), with opportunities for pony trekking, mountain biking and fishing. Welsh Royal Crystal Visitor Centre. Small museum. An interesting walk through the country on the nearby Gigrin Farm Trail.

Gd6   Sennybridge

Village between Brecon and Llandovery with the Brecon Beacons National Park to the south and the wild hills of Mynydd Eppynt to the north. Good touring centre for South and Mid Wales. Magnificent walking country on the doorstep.

Ec5   Welshpool

Old market town of the borderlands, full of character, with half-timbered buildings and welcoming inns. Attractive canalside museum. Good shopping centre; golf and angling. Powis Castle is an impressive stately home with a Clive of India Museum and outstanding gardens. Ride the narrow-gauge Welshpool and Llanfair Light Railway, visit the Moors Wildlife Collection.

Brecon

H	Tai'r Bull Inn

Libanus
Brecon
LD3 8EL
Tel: (01874) 625849

COMMENDED

Ideal walking and touring base; close to Mountain Centre, Pen-y-fan and Brecon, although situated in the small rural village of Libanus. Beautiful countryside surroundings with waterfalls, pony trekking and many attractions. All our rooms are en-suite and evening meal is available all week. Packed lunches on request. Private car park.

		SINGLE PER PERSON B&B	DOUBLE FOR 2 PERSONS B&B		5
					5
		MIN £	MAX £	MIN £	MAX £	OPEN
		-	-	36.00	36.00	1-12

GH	The Coach Guest House

Orchard Street
Brecon
LD3 8AN
Tel: (01874) 623803

 HIGHLY COMMENDED

"Hotel standards at guest house prices". Six bedrooms all en-suite, Three with bath, three with shower, Four double rooms, two twin. All have colour TV, hairdryer, clock radio, telephone and beverage tray. Whole house completely non smoking. Ideal base for touring Brecon Beacons National Park. Close to town centre. RAC Highly Acclaimed. AA Listed QQQQ.

		SINGLE PER PERSON B&B	DOUBLE FOR 2 PERSONS B&B		6
					6
		MIN £	MAX £	MIN £	MAX £	OPEN
		-	-	36.00	38.00	1-12

GH	The Old Rectory

Llanddew,
Brecon
LD3 9SS
Tel: (01874) 622058

HIGHLY COMMENDED

Peacefully situated in 2 acres of its own grounds. The Old Rectory is 1.5 miles from Brecon with magnificent views of the Brecon Beacons. Every comfort provided for, central heating, colour TV, tea/coffee in all rooms. A warm welcome is assured and personal service. Pony trekking, golf, fishing nearby. Ample parking. RAC Acclaimed.

		SINGLE PER PERSON B&B	DOUBLE FOR 2 PERSONS B&B		3
					2
		MIN £	MAX £	MIN £	MAX £	OPEN
		-	-	36.00	36.00	1-12

GH	The Beacons Guest House

16 Bridge Street
Brecon
LD3 8AH
Tel: (01874) 623339

 COMMENDED

A friendly atmosphere is assured in our Georgian guest house close to town centre, river and Brecon Beacons. En-suite rooms with beverage tray and colour TV. Cosy bar, residents lounge and private parking. Groups, pets and children welcome! Excellent home cooking - "Taste of Wales" recommended. Credit cards accepted. Please write or telephone for brochure.

		SINGLE PER PERSON B&B	DOUBLE FOR 2 PERSONS B&B		10
					7
		MIN £	MAX £	MIN £	MAX £	OPEN
		16.50	-	33.00	39.00	1-12

GH	Glanyrafon

The Promenade,
Kensington,
Brecon LD3 9AY
Tel: (01874) 623302

 HIGHLY COMMENDED

Elegant Edwardian residence set in quiet location on the Usk River bank, close to town centre and other amenities. Pleasant garden to sit in with view of Beacons. Vanity units and tea/coffee facilities in each bedroom. Comfortable guests' lounge with colour television. Friendly Welsh welcome assured. Siaredir Cymraeg.

		SINGLE PER PERSON B&B	DOUBLE FOR 2 PERSONS B&B		3
					-
		MIN £	MAX £	MIN £	MAX £	OPEN
		16.00	17.00	28.00	30.00	4-10

GH	Tir Bach Guest House

13 Alexandra Road,
Brecon
LD3 7PD
Tel: (01874) 624551

Comfortable, homely, family run guest house. On quiet road overlooking town. 2 minutes walk from town centre. Panoramic view of Brecon Beacons. Lounge with colour TV. Plentiful hot water, central heating, car parking, traditional British breakfast. Special rates for children. Well travelled friendly hosts. (No B&B sign on house).

		SINGLE PER PERSON B&B	DOUBLE FOR 2 PERSONS B&B		3
					-
		MIN £	MAX £	MIN £	MAX £	OPEN
		16.00	16.00	29.00	32.00	1-11

GH	Cambridge House

St David Street
Brecon
LD3 8BB
Tel: (01874) 624699

HIGHLY COMMENDED

Small quiet family run guest house close to town centre and the Beacons. Clean and cosy. Activities arranged. Our en-suite room is equipped with dressing table, hairdryer. Superb views of the Beacons. Full fire certificate, private parking. Pay phone, ironing facilities available. Packed lunches, evening meals. Full central heating, double glazed throughout. Brochure available.

		SINGLE PER PERSON B&B	DOUBLE FOR 2 PERSONS B&B		4
					1
		MIN £	MAX £	MIN £	MAX £	OPEN
		13.00	15.00	28.00	32.00	1-12

GH	Glascwm Guest House

Talyllyn,
Brecon
LD3 7SY
Tel: (01874) 658649

HIGHLY COMMENDED

Edwardian house set in 5 acres with nice views. Tea/coffee facilities, hot & cold in all rooms. Near lake, pony trekking, Big Pit Mining Museum, Brecon Beacons, Black Mountains, walking. En-suite available, parking. Take A40 towards abergavenny from Brecon for 1.5 miles, turn left at Llangorse, signpost on left. First right for 2 miles, see finger post on left pointing right to Talyllyn, take first right at bottom of hill.

		SINGLE PER PERSON B&B	DOUBLE FOR 2 PERSONS B&B		3
					2
		MIN £	MAX £	MIN £	MAX £	OPEN
		17.00	-	32.00	-	1-12

FH	Brynfedwen Farm

Trallong Common,
Sennybridge,
Brecon
LD3 8HW
Tel: (01874) 636505

 HIGHLY COMMENDED

Brynfedwen, meaning "hill of the birch trees", is a family farm set high above the Usk Valley commanding splendid views of the Brecon Beacons. Well situated for all country pursuits or just relaxing. Period, centrally heated farmhouse, all three rooms are en-suite, including self-contained flat, designed for disabled visitors. Good home cooking. Children welcome.

		SINGLE PER PERSON B&B	DOUBLE FOR 2 PERSONS B&B		3
					3
		MIN £	MAX £	MIN £	MAX £	OPEN
		17.00	-	34.00	-	1-12

Mid Wales Lakes and Mountains, the Brecon Beacons and More . . .

Brecon   Builth Wells

FH	Llanbrynean Farm

Llanfrynach,
Brecon
LD3 7BQ
Tel: (01874) 665222

Come and relax in the heart of the Brecon Beacons in our fine, period farmhouse with spacious accommodation and homely relaxed atmosphere. Situated on the edge of quiet, picturesque village offering excellent pub food. We have wonderful pastoral views and a large garden. Tea/coffee facilities, sitting room with log fire, TV. Working family farm.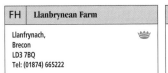

	SINGLE PER PERSON B&B		DOUBLE FOR 2 PERSONS B&B		🛏 3
					-
	MIN £	MAX £	MIN £	MAX £	OPEN
	16.00	17.00	2900	33.00	2-12

FH	Trehenry Farm

Felinfach,
Brecon
LD3 0UN
Tel: (01874) 754312

A 200 acre working farm east of Brecon. The impressive 18th century farmhouse with breathtaking views, inglenook fireplace, exposed beams offers select accommodation. Cosy rooms, TV lounge, central heating, separate tables. All rooms with TV, private bathroom, tea/coffee facilities. Personal service and good food is assured. Come and sample for yourself. Also self-catering farmhouse. Brochure on request

	SINGLE PER PERSON B&B		DOUBLE FOR 2 PERSONS B&B		🛏 3
					3
	MIN £	MAX £	MIN £	MAX £	OPEN
	-	-	36.00	38.00	1-12

GH	Old Vicarage Guest House

Erwood,
Builth Wells
LD2 3SZ
Tel: (01982) 560680

Beautiful setting just off A470 near Erwood. Breathtaking views, spacious attractive rooms with double aspects. Secluded position with period furniture and Victorian patchwork bedcovers, beverage tray, hand basins, full CH in bedrooms. Guests' own bathroom, separate WC, private TV lounge, indoor games, separate dining room. Traditional farmhouse roasts a speciality. Children, pets welcome. Elan Valley, Brecon Beacons, Hay-on-Wye, walks, trekking nearby.

	SINGLE PER PERSON B&B		DOUBLE FOR 2 PERSONS B&B		🛏 3
					-
	MIN £	MAX £	MIN £	MAX £	OPEN
	13.00	14.00	26.00	28.00	1-12

FH	LLwyncynog Farm

Felinfach,
Brecon
LD3 0UG
Tel: (01874) 623475

Situated in peaceful countryside, 5 miles east of Brecon. Glorious views of the Brecon Beacons and Black Mountains. 17th century farmhouse, with guests' lounge/dining room with colour TV & video. Comfortable bedrooms with beverage facilities. Family and twin rooms both en-suite, double room with private bathroom. Central for many leisure activities or quiet walks.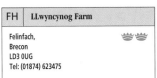

	SINGLE PER PERSON B&B		DOUBLE FOR 2 PERSONS B&B		🛏 3
					3
	MIN £	MAX £	MIN £	MAX £	OPEN
	14.00	15.00	28.00	30.00	4-10

FH	Upper Cantref Farm

Cantref,
Brecon LD3 8LR
Tel: (01874) 665223
Fax: (01874) 665223

Situated in the Brecon Beacons National Park on a genuine working farm with excellent views and within walking distance of the main peaks (Pen-y-Fan). Family run in a quiet location with comfortable and spacious bedrooms in traditional farmhouse. En-suite available. Pony trekking on site.

	SINGLE PER PERSON B&B		DOUBLE FOR 2 PERSONS B&B		🛏 2
					1
	MIN £	MAX £	MIN £	MAX £	OPEN
	-	-	28.00	36.00	4-11

GH	Querida

43 Garth Road,
Builth Wells
LD2 3AR
Tel: (01982) 553642

Querida, within easy reach of town centre with its sports field, swimming pool, golf, cricket etc. Royal Welsh Showground nearby. Ideal spot from which to tour Black Mountains, Brecon Beacons, Elan Valley and Hay on Wye. Many Welsh craft shops nearby. TV lounge, tea and coffee all rooms, wash basins, two toilets, bath and shower.

	SINGLE PER PERSON B&B		DOUBLE FOR 2 PERSONS B&B		🛏 2
					-
	MIN £	MAX £	MIN £	MAX £	OPEN
	13.00	15.00	26.00	30.00	1-12

FH	The Tower

Scethrog,
Brecon
LD3 7YE
Tel: (01874) 676672
Fax: (0181) 960 8246

COMMENDED

Romantic, medieval house surrounded by meadows, mountains and river. Two spacious oak beamed bed-sitting rooms, each with own en-suite toilet and wash basin, colour TV, fridge and tea/coffee. Picnic in large garden, overlooking kingfisher pond or around the fire in your own room. Relaxed atmosphere. Late breakfast. Steep stone steps. Private trout fishing.

	SINGLE PER PERSON B&B		DOUBLE FOR 2 PERSONS B&B		🛏 2
					-
	MIN £	MAX £	MIN £	MAX £	OPEN
	18.00	20.00	30.00	36.00	3-10

H	Griffin Inn

Cwm Owen,
Builth Wells
LD2 3HY
Tel: (01982) 558778

COMMENDED

Step back in time on an adventure into the past, enjoy a meal in our gas lit restaurant, or a draught ale in the stone flagged gas lit bar. All rooms en-suite, tea/coffee facilities and TV. Free fishing for residents in our own stocked pool. Nigel and Lana look forward to meeting you at the beginning of your adventure.

	SINGLE PER PERSON B&B		DOUBLE FOR 2 PERSONS B&B		🛏 3
					3
	MIN £	MAX £	MIN £	MAX £	OPEN
	20.00			36.00	1-12

FH	Caepandy Farm

Garth Road,
Builth Wells
LD2 3NS
Tel: (01982) 553793

L

A welcome awaits you at Caepandy Farm, modernised 17th century house with magnificent views across Irfon & Wye Valleys. One mile from Builth Wells, within easy reach of Elan Valley, Black Mountains, Breacon Beacons and Cambrian Mountains. Pony trekking, swimming, golf, cricket, sports hall, nearby. Tea & coffee all rooms. TV lounge.

	SINGLE PER PERSON B&B		DOUBLE FOR 2 PERSONS B&B		🛏 3
					-
	MIN £	MAX £	MIN £	MAX £	OPEN
	13.00	14.00	26.00	28.00	1-12

Builth Wells Crickhowell Erwood Felinfach Hay-on-Wye

FH	Dollynwydd Farm

Builth Wells
LD2 3RZ
Tel: (01982) 553660

 COMMENDED

17th century farmhouse in lovely quiet area lying beneath the Eppynt range of hills. Four bedrooms, 1 en-suite. Evening meal by arrangement. Home cooking. Oak beams, log fire. Very comfortable. Outstanding area for walking, birdwatching, touring. Elan Valley, Brecon Beacons, Black Mountains nearby. We are 1 mile from Builth Wells, B4520 first left, signed Tregare, Erwood, down farm lane. **i**

P	⦿	SINGLE PER PERSON B&B	DOUBLE FOR 2 PERSONS B&B	🛏	4
					1

MIN £	MAX £	MIN £	MAX £	OPEN
14.00	20.00	28.00	40.00	1-12

GH	The Firs

Tretower,
Crickhowell,
Brecon NP8 1RF
Tel: (01874) 730780

HIGHLY COMMENDED

300 year old country house with cottage style characteristics. Set in a secluded position at eastern side of Brecon Beacons National Park. Wonderful views. Good food and hospitality is of prime importance. Tea and coffee in bedrooms. Walks from our door step. **i**

P	🐕	SINGLE PER PERSON B&B	DOUBLE FOR 2 PERSONS B&B	🛏	4
					2

MIN £	MAX £	MIN £	MAX £	OPEN
-	-	38.00	40.00	1-12

FH	The Old Mill

Felinfach,
Brecon
LD3 0UB
Tel: (01874) 625385

Peacefully situated in its own grounds in the village of Felinfach, just 4.5 miles from Brecon. The Old Mill has a wealth of character, friendly atmosphere, large garden. TV lounge, tea/coffee facilities, two twin en-suite and one double with bathroom. Within easy reach of Brecon Beacons, Black Mountains, Hay-on-Wye, pony trekking, and within walking distance of local inn. **i**

P	🛏	SINGLE PER PERSON B&B	DOUBLE FOR 2 PERSONS B&B	🛏	3
					2

MIN £	MAX £	MIN £	MAX £	OPEN
16.00	18.00	28.00	32.00	3-11

FH	Ty-isaf Farm

Erwood,
Builth Wells
LD2 3SZ
Tel: (01982) 560607

 AWARD

Ty-isaf is a mixed working farm just off A470, near Erwood village, with beautiful views overlooking Wye Valley and surrounding countryside. Ideal spot for walking, touring Mid Wales, within easy reach of Elan Valley, Brecon Beacons National Park and Black Mountains. Fishing available. Tea & coffee all rooms. Guest TV lounge, farmhouse cooking. **i**

P	🐕	SINGLE PER PERSON B&B	DOUBLE FOR 2 PERSONS B&B	🛏	3
	⦿				-

MIN £	MAX £	MIN £	MAX £	OPEN
14.00	-	26.00	28.00	1-12

GH	White Hall

Glangrwyne,
Crickhowell
NP8 1EW
Tel: (01873) 811155

Comfortable accommodation in Georgian house in ideal walking country between Black Mountains and Brecon Beacons National Park. Canal trips, pony trekking, riding nearby. Also Norman castles, ancient churches, and industrial heritage (Big Pit and museums). Extensive library of books for all ages. Bank holidays, minimum 2 nights; reduced rates 3 nights or more. **i**

P	🐕	SINGLE PER PERSON B&B	DOUBLE FOR 2 PERSONS B&B	🛏	3
C					2

MIN £	MAX £	MIN £	MAX £	OPEN
20.00	20.00	15.00	20.00	1-12

GH	The Forge

Glasbury,
Near Hay-on-Wye HR3 5LN
Tel: (01497) 847237
Fax: (01497) 847237

Comfortable welcoming 17th century longhouse near River Wye beach. Satellite, trays, central heating in bedrooms. Activities arranged include canoeing, pony trekking. Plenty of wildlife in delightfully unspoilt countryside, near Black Mountains, Brecon Beacons, bookshops, superior restaurants. Quiet village location with shaded, sunny, secluded gardens. Dietary catering. Exotic birds and pets. Tourist literature. Parking. Relaxed atmosphere. Help with excursions. **i**

P	🐕	SINGLE PER PERSON B&B	DOUBLE FOR 2 PERSONS B&B	🛏	3
					2

MIN £	MAX £	MIN £	MAX £	OPEN
16.00	18.00	32.00	36.00	4-11

H	The Bell Inn

Glangrwyne,
Near Crickhowell
NP8 1EH
Tel: (01873) 810247

Delightful 17th century former coaching inn situated in the heart off the Usk Valley, in the Brecon Beacons National Park. Full of oak beams and character. Extensive à la carte menu and a reputation for excellent home cooked food. Some rooms en-suite, all with colour TV. Hang gliding, pony trekking, walking, sailing, fishing available, all nearby. Private fishing on the River Usk available. **i**

P	⦿	SINGLE PER PERSON B&B	DOUBLE FOR 2 PERSONS B&B	🛏	4
					1

MIN £	MAX £	MIN £	MAX £	OPEN
18.00	20.00	35.00	40.00	1-12

GH	Orchard Cottage

Erwood,
Builth Wells
LD2 3EZ
Tel: (01982) 560600

 HIGHLY COMMENDED

200 year old tastefully modernised cottage on banks of River Wye. Wonderful views. Good value evening meals at inn next door. Colour TV, tea/coffee facilities in all rooms. Cots and high chairs available. Fishing available in Cletwr Brook. Ideal centre for exploring Mid Wales. Nearby canoeing, horse riding, gliding, swimming, Local new sports centre. Homely welcome from well travelled hosts Pat and Alan Prior. **i**

P	🐕	SINGLE PER PERSON B&B	DOUBLE FOR 2 PERSONS B&B	🛏	3
					1

MIN £	MAX £	MIN £	MAX £	OPEN
18.00	-	31.00	36.00	1-12

GH	The Old Post Office

Llanigon,
Hay-on-Wye
HR3 5QA
Tel: (01497) 820008

COMMENDED

17th century character house in a quiet rural location, only two miles from the famous book town of Hay-on-Wye. Set in the lovely Brecon Beacons National Park at the foot of the Black Mountains. Offa's Dyke Path close by. Superb vegetarian breakfast early or late. Relaxed atmosphere. Guests' own sitting room and lovely bedrooms. **i**

P	🐕	SINGLE PER PERSON B&B	DOUBLE FOR 2 PERSONS B&B	🛏	3
					2

MIN £	MAX £	MIN £	MAX £	OPEN
-	-	30.00	38.00	2-12

Mid Wales Lakes and Mountains, the Brecon Beacons and More . . .

Hay-on-Wye   Llandrindod Wells   Llanfair Caereinion   Llangurig   Llanidloes   Llanwddyn

FH — Ffordd Fawr Farmhouse

Glasbury,
Hay-on-Wye
HR3 5PT
Tel: (01497) 847332

HIGHLY COMMENDED

Receive a friendly welcome and feel at home in this late 17th century farmhouse. Set in the Wye Valley with beautiful unspoilt countryside. Ideal for all country pursuits. Take A438 from Hereford to Glasbury. At T junction turn left onto B4350 towards Hay-on-Wye. First farm on left.

	SINGLE PER PERSON B&B	DOUBLE FOR 2 PERSONS B&B	🛏 3
			3
MIN £ 20.00	MAX £ 20.00	MIN £ 38.00	MAX £ 40.00	OPEN 3-11

FH — Brynhir Farm

Chapel Road,
Howey,
Llandrindod Wells
LD1 5PB
Tel: (01597) 822425

HIGHLY COMMENDED

Charming olde worlde farmhouse situated 1 mile off A483, in magnificent mountain setting. Traditional inglenook fireplace, exposed oak beams. Ideal relaxing holiday, good walking area. Trout fishing lake. Pied flycatchers, redstarts and buzzards commonly seen. Conducted badger sett tours. Beverage trays. Delicious cuisine. 1 mile off A483 through Howey village, turn right up Chapel Road. Evening meal by arrangement.

	SINGLE PER PERSON B&B	DOUBLE FOR 2 PERSONS B&B	🛏 6
			6
MIN £ 17.00	MAX £ 18.00	MIN £ 34.00	MAX £ 36.00	OPEN 3-11

GH — The Old Vicarage

Llangurig
SY18 6RN
Tel: (01686) 440280
Fax: (01686) 440280

HIGHLY COMMENDED

Charming Victorian vicarage in superb rural setting, close to Elan Valley and Plynlimon Hills. Ideal base for walking, touring the lakes and mountains of central Wales. Peaceful location in quiet cul-de-sac. All rooms en-suite with TV and tea/coffee facilities. Central heating. Log fires on colder evenings. Pets welcome. WTB award for comfort/service.

	SINGLE PER PERSON B&B	DOUBLE FOR 2 PERSONS B&B	🛏 3
			3
MIN £ -	MAX £ -	MIN £ 36.00	MAX £ 40.00	OPEN 3-10

GH — Corven Hall

Howey,
Llandrindod Wells
LD1 5RE
Tel: (01597) 823368

HIGHLY COMMENDED

Victorian country house in large grounds surrounded by beautiful countryside. 1.5 miles south of Llandrindod Wells, off A483 at Hundred House Turn. The house is licensed, centrally heated and spacious. TV lounge, bar. Most bedrooms en-suite, TV, tea/coffee facilities, ground floor accommodation. Traditional home cooking, freshly prepared. Dinners by arrangement. Brochure. Rod and Beryl Prince.

	SINGLE PER PERSON B&B	DOUBLE FOR 2 PERSONS B&B	🛏 10
			8
MIN £ 16.00	MAX £ 20.00	MIN £ 32.00	MAX £ 37.00	OPEN 2-10

FH — Holly Farm

Howey,
Llandrindod Wells
LD1 5PP
Tel: (01597) 822402

HIGHLY COMMENDED

Holly Farm, set in beautiful countryside, offers guests a friendly welcome. 1.5 miles south of Llandrindod Wells. Excellent base for exploring lakes, mountains, bird watching or just relaxing. Full central heating, en-suite rooms, beverage trays. TV lounge, log fire, dining room, separate tables. Superb meals, using home produce. Safe car parking, AA Listed. Evening meals by arrangement. Brochure, Mrs Ruth Jones.

	SINGLE PER PERSON B&B	DOUBLE FOR 2 PERSONS B&B	🛏 3
			3
MIN £ 18.00	MAX £ -	MIN £ 32.00	MAX £ 36.00	OPEN 4-11

FH — Esgairmaen y Fan

Llanidloes
SY18 6NT
Tel: (01686) 430272

Esgairmaen is a farmhouse situated 1 mile from the Clywedog Reservoir, where fishing and sailing can be enjoyed. An ideal base for walking, bird watching and exploring nearby forests. The farmhouse commands magnificent views and the atmosphere is peaceful. Guests can be sure of a warm welcome.

	SINGLE PER PERSON B&B	DOUBLE FOR 2 PERSONS B&B	🛏 2
			2
MIN £ 16.00	MAX £ 18.00	MIN £ 28.00	MAX £ 32.00	OPEN 1-10

GH — Ty-Clyd Guest House

Park Terrace,
Llandrindod Wells
LD1 6AY
Tel: (01597) 822122

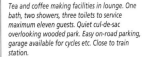

Tea and coffee making facilities in lounge. One bath, two showers, three toilets to service maximum eleven guests. Quiet cul-de-sac overlooking wooded park. Easy on-road parking, garage available for cycles etc. Close to train station.

	SINGLE PER PERSON B&B	DOUBLE FOR 2 PERSONS B&B	🛏 7
			-
MIN £ 14.00	MAX £ 14.00	MIN £ 28.00	MAX £ 28.00	OPEN 1-12

FH — Madog's Wells

Llanfair Caereinion,
Welshpool
SY21 0DE
Tel: (01938) 810446

Small hill farm in beautiful secluded valley. Ideal for touring Mid Wales. Wash basins, tea/coffee in all rooms, visitors' bathroom. Reduced rates for under 12's. TV, games room. Also two fully equipped 6/8 berth caravans, maximum £160 pw. bungalow sleeps 3, disabled criteria 2, maximum £220. Astronomical observatory with superb 16" Dobsonian telescope, with NGC max computer.

	SINGLE PER PERSON B&B	DOUBLE FOR 2 PERSONS B&B	🛏 2
			2
MIN £ 14.00	MAX £ 14.00	MIN £ -	MAX £ 28.00	OPEN 1-12

FH — Tynymaes

Llanwddyn
SY10 0NN
Tel: (01691) 870216

HIGHLY COMMENDED

Croeso cynnes. A warm welcome awaits you at Tynymaes, a working farm situated 2 miles from the peace and tranquillity of Lake Vyrnwy and the RSPB reserve. Magnificent views and ideal for walking and touring. Scenic mountain drives to Bala and the surrounding countryside. Homely atmosphere and good traditional home cooking. Enquiries to H A Parry.

	SINGLE PER PERSON B&B	DOUBLE FOR 2 PERSONS B&B	🛏 3
			0
MIN £ 16.00	MAX £ 16.00	MIN £ 30.00	MAX £ 32.00	OPEN 5-10

Llanwrtyd Wells Montgomery Newtown Penybontfawr Presteigne

GH	Cerdyn Country Guest House

Cerdyn Villa,
Llanwrtyd Wells LD5 4RS
Tel: (01591) 610635
Fax: (01591) 610666

Peaceful location amongst mountains, lakes, rivers and forests. Family run guest house in large Victorian house with comfortable accommodation, log fires and plentiful good home cooked food. Spectacular walking, cycling, riding, birdwatching. Special rates for groups (8+), short breaks. Self-contained apartment within 200 yards. 0.5 miles from A483, BR station 200 yards. ℹ️

P	C	SINGLE PER PERSON B&B	DOUBLE FOR 2 PERSONS B&B	🛏 4
🛏 ✕ 🍽				🛁 2

MIN £	MAX £	MIN £	MAX £	OPEN
-	-	30.00	36.00	1-12

GH	Greenfields

Kerry,
Newtown SY16 4LH
Tel: (01686) 670596
Fax: (01686) 670354

*A warm welcome awaits you at our home. The spacious bedrooms have picturesque views of the rolling hills of Kerry. The lounge has an open log fire and the dining room has separate tables. Greenfields is an excellent stopping place for one night stops, weekends or longer breaks while exploring Mid Wales and borderlands.
Your contact is Vi Madeley.* ℹ️

P	🐕	SINGLE PER PERSON B&B	DOUBLE FOR 2 PERSONS B&B	🛏 3
🛏 ✕				🛁 3

MIN £	MAX £	MIN £	MAX £	OPEN
14.00	17.00	34.00	38.00	1-12

FH	Glanhafon

COMMENDED

Penybontfawr,
Oswestry
SY10 0EW
Tel: (01691) 860377

Secluded farmhouse in the upper Tanat Valley, close to Lake Vyrnwy and Pistyll Falls. A working sheep farm, with rock climbing and hill walks on farm. One twin, private bathroom. Double and family en-suite, own sitting room with log fire. Central heating. Children welcome. Brochure and enquires to Anne Evans. ℹ️

P	🐕	SINGLE PER PERSON B&B	DOUBLE FOR 2 PERSONS B&B	🛏 3
🛏 ✕				🛁 3

MIN £	MAX £	MIN £	MAX £	OPEN
14.00	18.00	28.00	28.00	4-11

FH	The Drewin Farm

HIGHLY COMMENDED

Churchstoke,
Montgomery
SY15 6TW
Tel: (01588) 620325

This friendly, family run farmhouse was featured on BBC Travel Show 1993. With panoramic views, bedrooms have TV, hairdryer and drinks facilities. En-suite available. Games room with snooker table. Good home cooking is served in the oak beamed dining room, vegetarian by request. Offa's Dyke Path runs through farm. A warm welcome awaits. AA Selected. ℹ️

P	🐕	SINGLE PER PERSON B&B	DOUBLE FOR 2 PERSONS B&B	🛏 2
🛏 ✕ 🍽				🛁 1

MIN £	MAX £	MIN £	MAX £	OPEN
18.00	20.00	30.00	34.00	4-10

FH	Lower-Gwestydd

HIGHLY COMMENDED

Llanllwchaiarn,
Newtown
SY16 3AY
Tel: (01686) 626718

Beautiful 17th century listed farmhouse set just off the B4568 north of Newtown. Two rooms en-suite, all centrally heated, tea/coffee making facilities. Separate dining room. Lounge with colour TV. Large garden providing produce for the table. Lovely views from this 200 acre farm. A warm welcome to all. ℹ️

P	🛏	SINGLE PER PERSON B&B	DOUBLE FOR 2 PERSONS B&B	🛏 2
🍽				🛁 2

MIN £	MAX £	MIN £	MAX £	OPEN
18.00	18.50	34.00	35.00	1-12

FH	Penyceunant

HIGHLY COMMENDED

Penybontfawr
SY10 0PF
Tel: (01691) 860459

Old farmhouse with spectacular views across the Tanat Valley. Substantial rooms with wash basin, colour TV and easy chair. Guests' garden lounge. Ideal as a secluded retreat yet well placed for touring. We specialise in walking holidays, offering half board packages for week long or weekend breaks. Information service, route card loan. Enquiries, brochure - Anna Francis. ℹ️

P	🛏	SINGLE PER PERSON B&B	DOUBLE FOR 2 PERSONS B&B	🛏 2
✕ 🍽				🛁 -

MIN £	MAX £	MIN £	MAX £	OPEN
17.00	17.00	29.00	29.00	1-11

FH	Little Brompton Farm

HIGHLY COMMENDED

Montgomery
SY15 6HY
Tel: (01686) 668371

Charming 17th century farmhouse on working farm situated on B4385 two miles east of Montgomery, 0.5 miles west of A489. Traditionally furnished. En-suite rooms available. Delicious home cooking. Central heating. Pretty rooms enhanced by quality furnishings and antiques. Offa's Dyke Path runs through farm. Offering friendly and relaxed atmosphere. Open all year. AA QQQQ Selected. Mrs G Bright. ℹ️

P	🐕	SINGLE PER PERSON B&B	DOUBLE FOR 2 PERSONS B&B	🛏 3
🛏 ✕ 🍽				🛁 3

MIN £	MAX £	MIN £	MAX £	OPEN
18.00	19.00	38.00	40.00	1-12

FH	Dyffryn

DE LUXE

Aberhafesp,
Newtown SY16 3JD
Tel: (01686) 688817
Mobile: (0585) 206412
Fax: (01686) 688324

Luxury accommodation in 17th century restored barn, set on a working farm. En-suite rooms with TV's and central heating. Guest lounge and dining room. Delicious farmhouse fare including vegetarian. Lovely walks alone the stream in the woodland and nearby hills. Warm welcome guaranteed by Sue who was runner-up in the AA Landlady of the Year Competition 1995 ℹ️

P	🛏	SINGLE PER PERSON B&B	DOUBLE FOR 2 PERSONS B&B	🛏 3
✕ 🍽				🛁 3

MIN £	MAX £	MIN £	MAX £	OPEN
20.00	24.00	38.00	44.00	1-12

FH	Willey Lodge Farm

COMMENDED

Presteigne
LD8 2NB
Tel: (01544) 267341

Relax in our 16th century black and white farmhouse in beautiful border country, the heart of the Marches, close to Offa's Dyke, historic Ludlow, Hay and the books. Perfect for walking, touring or staying at home. Private facilities, visitors' separate dining and sitting rooms. Children welcome. Reduced rates. Contact Anne Davies. ℹ️

P	🐕	SINGLE PER PERSON B&B	DOUBLE FOR 2 PERSONS B&B	🛏 2
🛏 ✕ 🍽				🛁 1

MIN £	MAX £	MIN £	MAX £	OPEN
15.00	15.00	28.00	30.00	3-11

Mid Wales Lakes and Mountains, the Brecon Beacons and More . . .

Rhayader   Sennybridge   Welshpool

GH Brynteg

East Street,
Rhayader
LD6 5EA
Tel: (01597) 810052

Friendly Edwardian guest house overlooking hills and gardens, close to town centre. We have double, twin or single rooms with en-suite, central heating, tea/coffee facilities, TV lounge and separate breakfast room. Special rates for 4 nights or more. Children half price. We are ideally situated for exploring the Elan Valley Lakes and Cambrian Mountains. Croeso.

	SINGLE PER PERSON B&B	DOUBLE FOR 2 PERSONS B&B		4
				4
MIN £	MAX £	MIN £	MAX £	OPEN
14.50	14.50	29.00	29.00	1-12

FH Gigrin Farm

South Road,
Rhayader
LD6 5BL
Tel: (01597) 810243

Gigrin is a 17th century longhouse peacefully situated overlooking the Wye Valley, only 0.5 miles from Rhayader with its numerous inns and friendly welcome. The spectacular Elan Valley, home of the red kite is just 3 miles away. Aberystwyth 35 miles away. Our working farm offers a nature trail, RSPB Reserve and fishing. Walking, pony trekking and golf are available nearby. Three bedrooms.

	SINGLE PER PERSON B&B	DOUBLE FOR 2 PERSONS B&B		3
				1
MIN £	MAX £	MIN £	MAX £	OPEN
16.00	20.00	30.00	40.00	1-12

FH Plasdwpa Farm

Berriew,
Welshpool
SY21 8PS
Tel: (01686) 640298

Dairy farm set 1.5 miles above the pretty village of Berriew. Sensational views over the Severn Valley and Shropshire Borders, seen from every room. Very central for touring and local attractions. Large bathroom with bath and shower. Every room has washbasin, colour TV and drinks facilities; one has balcony. All are nicely furnished. Children welcome.

	SINGLE PER PERSON B&B	DOUBLE FOR 2 PERSONS B&B		3
				-
MIN £	MAX £	MIN £	MAX £	OPEN
15.00	15.00	30.00	30.00	3-10

GH Liverpool House

East Street,
Rhayader
LD6 5EA
Tel: (01597) 810706

A warm welcome awaits you at Liverpool House where friendliness and service go hand in hand. Secure private car parking on premises. Bedrooms have colour television, clock radio, hairdryer, iron, beverage tray and most are en-suite. Full central heating. Spacious lounge. Reduced rates for children sharing with parents. Cot and highchair. Full fire certificate.

	SINGLE PER PERSON B&B	DOUBLE FOR 2 PERSONS B&B		4
				3
MIN £	MAX £	MIN £	MAX £	OPEN
15.00	-	27.00	-	1-12

FH Trephilip Farm

Sennybridge,
Brecon
LD3 8SA
Tel: (01874) 636610

HIGHLY COMMENDED

Georgian farmhouse in the heart of Brecon Beacons National Park. 0.75 miles off A40, 0.5 miles off A4067. En-suite facilities, tea/coffee tray. Guests' lounge with colour television and log fire. Private fishing. Short riverside walk to village restaurant and country pub, both serving excellent food. Ideally located for touring and exploring in unspoilt countryside.

	SINGLE PER PERSON B&B	DOUBLE FOR 2 PERSONS B&B		2
				1
MIN £	MAX £	MIN £	MAX £	OPEN
-	-	32.00	34.00	1-12

FH Tynllwyn Farm

Welshpool
SY21 9BW
Tel: (01938) 553175

Tynllwyn is a family farm and farmhouse with a friendly welcome. Good farmhouse food and bar licence. All bedrooms have central heating, colour TV, tea and coffee facilities, hot and cold wash units. 1 mile from lovely market town of Welshpool on the A490 north. Very quiet and pleasantly situated on a hillside with beautiful views. 2 day short bargain break available October - March. Pets by arrangement. "Taste of Wales" member.

	SINGLE PER PERSON B&B	DOUBLE FOR 2 PERSONS B&B		5
				-
MIN £	MAX £	MIN £	MAX £	OPEN
15.00	-	30.00	-	1-12

FH Downfield Farm

Rhayader
LD6 5PA
Tel: (01597) 810394

Welcome to Downfield, situated one mile east of Rhayader on the A44 road. 3 double bedrooms, all with hot and cold water, plug, beverage tray. Two bathrooms, one with shower. Lounge with television, dining room with separate tables. Fully centrally heated. Surrounded by hills and lakes. Ideal for touring, walking, bird watching etc.

	SINGLE PER PERSON B&B	DOUBLE FOR 2 PERSONS B&B		3
				-
MIN £	MAX £	MIN £	MAX £	OPEN
15.00	16.00	28.00	30.00	2-11

GH Peniarth

10 Cefn Hawys (off Adelaide Drive),
Red Bank,
Welshpool SY21 7RH
Tel: (01938) 552324

A warm friendly welcome awaits you. Detached house situated at the end of a quiet cul-de-sac on the outskirts of a small market town. No smoking. Special rates for children. Parking, central heating, TV, tea/coffee facilities. One of the bedrooms is en-suite. Ideal for walking and touring. Contact Heulwen Jones.

	SINGLE PER PERSON B&B	DOUBLE FOR 2 PERSONS B&B		3
				1
MIN £	MAX £	MIN £	MAX £	OPEN
14.00	14.00	28.00	34.00	4-10

Welcome Host

Customer care is our top priority.

It's what our Welcome Host scheme is all about. Welcome Host badge or certificate holders are part of a tradition of friendliness. The Welcome Host programme, which is open to everyone from hotel staff to taxi drivers, places the emphasis on warm Welsh hospitality and first-class service.

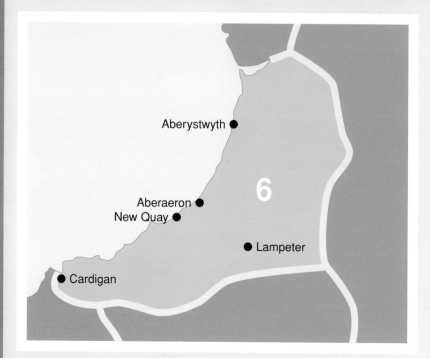

6

Aberystwyth ●

Aberaeron ●
New Quay ●

● Lampeter

● Cardigan

The southern arc of Cardigan Bay is dotted with pretty little ports and resorts, the largest of which is Victorian Aberystwyth with its splendid seafront. Long sections of this seashore have been designated Heritage Coast, including the exposed headland of Ynys Lochtyn near Llangrannog where on stormy days it almost seems as if you are sailing away from the mainland on board a ship. Inland, you'll discover traditional farming country matched by traditional country towns. Venture a little further and you'll come to the Cambrian Mountains, a compelling wilderness area crossed only by the occasional mountain road. The Teifi Valley, in contrast, is a gentle, leafy landscape famous for its beautiful river scenery, falls and coracle fishing.

It's a fact...

Dylan Thomas took much of his inspiration for the fictitious seatown of Llareggub in *Under Milk Wood* from New Quay. Remote Strata Florida Abbey, Pontrhydfendigaid, was known as the 'Westminster Abbey of Wales' in medieval times. Aberystwyth's Cliff Railway, opened in 1896, is Britain's longest electric-powered cliff railway. The scenic Teifi Valley was once Wales's busiest woollen making area – a few mills still survive. The coracle, a tiny, one-man fishing boat used in Wales for 2000 years, can still be seen on the waters of the Teifi.

Fc4   Aberaeron

Most attractive little town on Cardigan Bay, with distinctive Georgian-style architecture. Pleasant harbour, marine aquarium, coastal centre. Sailing popular, good touring centre for coast and country.

Fe2   Aberystwyth

Premier resort on the Cardigan Bay coastline. Fine promenade, cliff railway, camera obscura, harbour and many other seaside attractions. Excellent museum in restored Edwardian theatre. University town, lively arts centre with theatre and concert hall. National Library of Wales stands commandingly on hillside. Good shopping. Vale of Rheidol narrow-gauge steam line runs to Devil's Bridge falls.

Fa5   Cardigan

Market town on mouth of River Teifi close to beaches and resorts. Good shopping facilities, accommodation, inns. Golf and fishing. Base for exploring inland along wooded Teifi Valley and west to the Pembrokeshire Coast National Park. Y Felin Corn Mill and ruined abbey at neighbouring St Dogmael's. Welsh Wildlife Centre nearby.

Fa6   Cilgerran

Peaceful Teifiside village near Cardigan. Romantic ruins of Cilgerran Castle look down over river – coracles can sometimes be seen in the waters. Welsh Wildlife Centre on fringes of village.

Fe5   Lampeter

Farmers and students mingle in this distinctive small country town in the picturesque Teifi Valley. Concerts are often held in St David's University College, and visitors are welcome. Golf and angling, range of small shops and some old inns. Visit the landscaped Cae Hir Gardens, Cribyn.

Fc4   New Quay

Picturesque little resort with old harbour on Cardigan Bay. Lovely beaches and coves around and about. Good for sailing and fishing. Resort sheltered by protective headland.

New Quay

Aberaeron   Aberystwyth

GH	Hazeldene

South Road,
Aberaeron
SA46 0DP
Tel: (01545) 570652

A warm welcome with good home cooking awaits you. Enjoy this unique house with all comforts. Bedrooms en-suite; tea making facilities, colour televisions, one with king size water bed. Sky television, jacuzzi, fitness area, private sunbathing garden available. Fishing, riverside walks, tennis courts, children's playground, swimming pool, bowling club, harbour and sea front nearby. Croeso cynnes iawn.

P 🏠 ✖ 🍽	SINGLE PER PERSON B&B	DOUBLE FOR 2 PERSONS B&B	🛏 3 🛁 3
MIN £ 17.50	MAX £ 19.00	MIN £ 33.00	MAX £ 36.00	OPEN 5-9

Visitor's Guides to Mid Wales

In full colour and packed with information – a must for all visitors to Mid Wales
• Where to go and what to see •
Descriptions of towns, villages and resorts
• Hundreds of attractions and places to visit •
Detailed maps and town plans
• Scenic drives, beaches, narrow-gauge railways, what to do on a rainy day

£3.55 inc. p&p

(see 'Get Yourself a Guide' at the end of the book)

GH	Pantgwyn

Llanfarian,
Aberystwyth
SY23 4DE
Tel: (01970) 612031

This family run guest house is quietly situated in rural countryside in its own five acres of grounds. On the A487, just outside the village of Llanfarian. Private parking. All rooms have hot and cold, colour TV, tea/coffee making facilities, central heating. Some rooms en-suite. Ideal for a touring or relaxing holiday.

P 🐕 🏠	SINGLE PER PERSON B&B	DOUBLE FOR 2 PERSONS B&B	🛏 3 🛁 2
MIN £ 15.00	MAX £ 19.00	MIN £ 30.00	MAX £ 38.00	OPEN 1-12

GH	Llys Aeron Guest House

Lampeter Road,
Aberaeron
SA46 0ED
Tel: (01545) 570276

Spacious Georgian house. Breakfast room overlooking garden. All rooms H&C. Private forecourt parking. A lovely area to spend a relaxing holiday.

P 🐕 🏠	SINGLE PER PERSON B&B	DOUBLE FOR 2 PERSONS B&B	🛏 3 🛁 -
MIN £ 16.00	MAX £ 18.00	MIN £ 28.00	MAX £ 32.00	OPEN 1-12

H	The Halfway Inn

Devil's Bridge Road (A4120),
Pisgah,
Aberystwyth SY23 4NE
Tel: (01970) 880631

HIGHLY COMMENDED

Halfway between Aberystwyth and Devil's Bridge, 700 feet up on the A4120. This traditional hostelry is famous for its real ales and fine food. Relax in old fashioned ambience of flagstone floors, log fires and candles. Extensive grounds with magnificent views of the Rheidol Valley. Outdoor pursuits in the heart of red kite country.

P 🍷 🏠 🍽	SINGLE PER PERSON B&B	DOUBLE FOR 2 PERSONS B&B	🛏 2 🛁 2
MIN £ -	MAX £ -	MIN £ 39.00	MAX £ 39.00	OPEN 1-12

FH	Tycam Farm

Capel Bangor,
Aberystwyth
SY23 3NA
Tel: (01970) 880662

Peaceful dairy and sheep farm in glorious Rheidol Valley. 7.5 miles Aberystwyth, 2.5 miles off A44. Real home comforts are offered in traditional Cardiganshire farmhouse. Lounge, dining room, separate tables, colour TV. Perfect walking, bird watching, sightseeing 0.5 miles. Superb salmon, sewin, trout fishing on farm plus nearby lakes. Golf.

P 🏠 ⚒	SINGLE PER PERSON B&B	DOUBLE FOR 2 PERSONS B&B	🛏 2 🛁 2
MIN £ -	MAX £ -	MIN £ 32.00	MAX £ 36.00	OPEN 4-9

GH	Meysydd

Rhiwgoch,
Ffosyffin,
Aberaeron SA46 0EY
Tel: (01545) 571486

HIGHLY COMMENDED

A warm welcome awaits you at Meysydd, which is newly built, offering immaculate en-suite rooms. Completely non smoking. Television lounge, tea and coffee making facilities. Near Aberaeron in quiet location within easy reach of all amenities. Private parking. Within walking distance of village pub. Ideal base for touring beautiful coast and countryside of Mid Wales.

P 🏠 ✖	SINGLE PER PERSON B&B	DOUBLE FOR 2 PERSONS B&B	🛏 2 🛁 2
MIN £ -	MAX £ -	MIN £ 32.00	MAX £ 36.00	OPEN 4-9

H	Southgate Hotel

Antaron Avenue,
Penparcau,
Aberystwyth SY23 1SF
Tel: (01970) 611550

Small licensed hotel approximately one mile from town on the A487 Cardigan road. Double, family and twin rooms, en-suite available, with TV and tea/coffee facilities. Dinner optional. Ample parking in own grounds. Two ground floor bedrooms.

P 🏠 C 🍷 🏠 🍽	SINGLE PER PERSON B&B	DOUBLE FOR 2 PERSONS B&B	🛏 10 🛁 9
MIN £ -	MAX £ -	MIN £ 31.00	MAX £ 40.00	OPEN 2-12

Please Note

All the accommodation in this guide has applied for verification/classification and in many instances for grading also. However, at the time of going to press not all establishments had been visited – some of these properties are indicated by the wording 'Awaiting Inspection' or 'Awaiting Grading'.

GH Berwyn Guest House

St Dogmaels,
Cardigan
SA43 3HS
Tel: (01239) 613555

HIGHLY COMMENDED

Privately situated in 2 acres of delightful grounds with magnificent views overlooking Teifi River. Ideal centre for a relaxing holiday. Beautiful coast and countryside. All bedrooms have vanity suites, tea/coffee facilities. En-suite with private entrance to grounds. Colour TV, guest lounge, payphone, CH. Enjoy breakfast with gorgeous views. Private parking. Warm Welsh welcome to Berwyn. *i*

		SINGLE PER PERSON B&B	DOUBLE FOR 2 PERSONS B&B		3
P	⛟				2
MIN £ 16.50	MAX £ 19.00	MIN £ 29.00	MAX £ 38.00	OPEN 1-12	

GH Cartref

High Street,
Cilgerran,
Cardigan SA43 2SQ
Tel: (01239) 614479

AWAITING INSPECTION

I have a private house, with 2 double bedrooms and 1 single available for letting. 1 good sized bathroom with shower/bath. Lounge/diner 26 foot long. Good sized garden. Parking for cars in front of house.

		SINGLE PER PERSON B&B	DOUBLE FOR 2 PERSONS B&B		4
P	C				-
MIN £ 15.00	MAX £ 18.00	MIN £ 25.00	MAX £ 30.00	OPEN 1-12	

FH Brynog Mansion

Felinfach,
Lampeter
SA48 8AQ
Tel: (01570) 470266

HIGHLY COMMENDED

Spacious 250 year old mansion. Situated in the beautiful Vale of Aeron, midway between Lampeter University town and the unique Aberaeron seaside resort, 15 minutes by car. Approached by 0.75 miles rhododendron lined drive off the A482 main road and village of Felinfach. 2 spacious en-suite bedrooms, other near bathroom, tea making facilities, central heating. Full breakfast served in the grand old furnished dining room. *i*

		SINGLE PER PERSON B&B	DOUBLE FOR 2 PERSONS B&B		3
P	⛟				2
MIN £ 16.50	MAX £ 18.00	MIN £ 33.00	MAX £ 36.00	OPEN 1-12	

GH Brynhyfryd Guest House

Gwbert Road,
Cardigan
SA43 1AE
Tel: (01239) 612861
Fax: (01239) 612861

  HIGHLY COMMENDED

Situated in a pleasant area of the town, within two miles of Cardigan Bay. All bedrooms have colour television and tea/coffee facilities, en-suites available. Guests' lounge, evening meals, central heating, easy parking, fire certificate. AA Recommended and RAC Acclaimed. A high standard of comfort, cleanliness and good food is assured. Established 1980. Nesta & Ieuan Davies. *i*

	SINGLE PER PERSON B&B	DOUBLE FOR 2 PERSONS B&B		7
⛟				3
MIN £ 15.00	MAX £ 16.00	MIN £ 30.00	MAX £ 36.00	OPEN 1-12

FH Bryncastell Farm House

Llanfair Road,
Lampeter
SA48 8JY
Tel: (01570) 422447

HIGHLY COMMENDED

Bilingual Welsh family on 140 acre riverside farm. Panoramic views of Teifi Valley. Excellent cuisine featuring authentic Welsh recipes and home made wines. Combine traditional Welsh hospitality with comfort of modern conveniences. One mile from Lampeter town centre. 0.5 miles from Pioneer Co-op store. Signposted Llanfair Clydogau. Opposite W D Lewis Agricultural Merchants. "Taste of Wales" member. *i*

		SINGLE PER PERSON B&B	DOUBLE FOR 2 PERSONS B&B		3
P	C				2
MIN £ 16.50	MAX £ 18.00	MIN £ 33.00	MAX £ 35.00	OPEN 1-12	

H Tŷ Hen Farm Hotel and Cottages

Llwyndafydd,
New Quay
SA44 6BZ
Tel: (01545) 560346
Fax: (01545) 560346

Tŷ Hen is a peaceful working farm offering a choice of Self-catering Cottages or Bed and Breakfast and a private leisure centre with a large indoor heated swimming pool, sauna, sunbed, fitness-centre, skittles, table tennis and pool table. Licensed restaurant open on some evenings. Smoking only in cottages. Specialists in teaching the nervous adult to swim. *i*

		SINGLE PER PERSON B&B	DOUBLE FOR 2 PERSONS B&B		4
P					4
MIN £ 20.00	MAX £ 29.00	MIN £ 40.00	MAX £ -	OPEN 2-11	

Aberystwyth

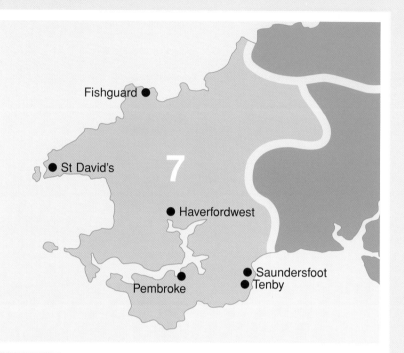

Pembrokeshire is traditionally known as *gwlad hud a lledrith*, 'the land of magic and enchantment'. Anyone who has visited the sandy bays around Tenby, for example, or the breathtaking sea-cliffs at Stack Rocks, or the rugged coastline around St David's will agree with this description. Pembrokeshire is one of Europe's finest stretches of coastal natural beauty. Not surprisingly, it's also a haven for wildlife. Wildflowers grow on its cliffs, seals swim in its clear waters, and seabirds nest in huge numbers all along the coast. Pembrokeshire's stunning coastal beauty extends inland to the Preseli Hills, an open expanse of highland scattered with mysterious prehistoric sites. And away from the coast you'll also discover castles and a host of places to visit.

It's a fact...

The Pembrokeshire Coast National Park covers 225 square miles and runs from Poppit Sands near Cardigan in the north to Amroth in the south. It was created in 1952. The park's symbol is the razorbill, a reflection of the prolific seabird populations to be found here. The Pembrokeshire Coast Path, opened in 1970, runs for 186 miles. The park's boundary clings to the coast except in one instance, when it dips inland to encompass the Preseli Hills, which rise to 536m/1760ft. The Dale Peninsula is the sunniest place in Wales.

Jb5 Broad Haven

Sand and green hills cradle this holiday village on St Bride's Bay in the Pembrokeshire Coast National Park. Beautiful beach and coastal walks. National Park Information Centre.

Jb3 Croes-goch

Small village, useful spot for touring Pembrokeshire Coast National Park – especially its peaceful, rugged northern shores and nearby centres of St David's and Fishguard. Llangloffan Farmhouse Cheese Centre nearby.

Jc2 Fishguard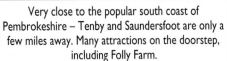

Lower Fishguard is a cluster of old wharfs and cottages around a beautiful harbour. *Under Milk Wood* with Richard Burton was filmed here in 1971. Shopping in Fishguard town. Good walks along Pembrokeshire Coast Path and in the country. Nearby Goodwick is the Irish ferry terminal, with a direct link from London. Excellent range of craft workshops in area including Tregwynt Woollen Mill. Music Festival in July.

Jd6 Freshwater East

Sheltered sandy bay south-east of Pembroke backed by dunes. Good swimming, access for boats, limited car parking.

Jc5 Haverfordwest

Ancient town – now a good base for exploring the Pembrokeshire Coast National Park – and the administrative and shopping centre for the area. Medieval churches and narrow streets. Museum in the castle grounds, which occupy an outcrop overlooking the town. Attractive redeveloped riverside and old wharf buildings. Picton Castle a few miles to the east. Many other attractions nearby, including Scolton Manor Country Park, 'Motormania' exhibition, Selvedge Farm Museum and Nant-y-Coy Mill.

Je5 Kilgetty

Very close to the popular south coast of Pembrokeshire – Tenby and Saundersfoot are only a few miles away. Many attractions on the doorstep, including Folly Farm.

Jb5 Little Haven

Combines with Broad Haven – just over the headland – to form a complete family seaside holiday centre in the Pembrokeshire Coast National Park. The village dips down to a pretty sandy beach. Popular spot for sailing, swimming and surfing.

Ka1 Llanfyrnach

Village in maze of peaceful, unexplored country lanes between Carmarthen and Cardigan. Handy for Pembrokeshire's north coast and Preseli Hills as well as Teifi Valley.

Je3 Maenclochog

Village on southern approach to Preseli Hills. Good touring centre for north and South Pembrokeshire. Preseli's prehistoric sites close by; Llys-y-fran Country Park, based around an attractive reservoir, a few miles to the south-west.

Jd2 Newport

Ancient castled village on Pembrokeshire coast. Fine beaches – bass and sea trout fishing. Pentre Ifan Burial Chamber is close by. Backed by heather-clad Preseli Hills and overlooked by Carn Ingli Iron Age Fort.

Broad Haven

Jd6   Pembroke

Ancient borough built around Pembroke Castle, birthplace of Henry VII. In addition to its impressive castle, well-preserved sections of old town walls. Fascinating Museum of the Home. Sandy bays within easy reach, yachting, fishing – all the coastal activities associated with estuaries. Plenty of things to see and do in the area, including visit to beautiful Upton Castle Grounds.

Ja4   St David's

Smallest cathedral city in Britain, shrine of Wales's patron saint. Magnificent ruins of a Bishop's Palace beside ancient cathedral nestling in hollow. Set in Pembrokeshire Coast National Park, with fine beaches nearby; superb scenery on nearby headland. Craft shops, sea life centres, painting courses, boat trips to Ramsey Island, farm parks and museums; ideal for walking and birdwatching.

Je6   St Florence

South Pembrokeshire village, in the country but only a stone's throw from popular Tenby. Some of Britain's most beautiful coastline on doorstep – Manorbier with its beach-side castle, Stackpole and Barafundle Bay. Local attractions include Folly Farm and Manor House Wildlife and Leisure Park.

Jb6   St Ishmael's

Village in far-flung south-west of the Pembrokeshire Coast National Park, close to sailing centre of Dale on the Milford Haven waterway. Some of Pembrokeshire's loveliest coastline close by – the unexplored Dale Peninsula, Marloes Sands, and boat trips to Skomer Island from Martin's Haven.

Je6   Saundersfoot

Popular resort on south Pembrokeshire coast within the National Park. Picturesque harbour and sandy beach. Very attractive sailing centre. Good sea fishing. In the wooded hills to the north is the fascinating Stepaside Industrial Heritage Centre.

Jb4   Solva

Pretty Pembrokeshire coast village with small perfectly sheltered harbour and excellent craft shops. Pembrokeshire Coast Path offers good walking. Famous cathedral at nearby St David's.

Je6   Tenby

Popular, picturesque south Pembrokeshire resort with two wide beaches. Fishing trips from the attractive Georgian harbour and boat trips to nearby Caldy Island. The medieval walled town has a maze of charming narrow streets and fine old buildings, including Tudor Merchant's House (National Trust). Galleries and craft shops, excellent museum on headland, good range of amenities. Attractions include Manor House Wildlife and Leisure Park and 'Silent World' Aquarium.

Solva harbour

Broad Haven Croes-goch Fishguard Freshwater East Haverfordwest

---

GH	Barley Villa

Walwyn's Castle,
Broad Haven,
Haverfordwest SA62 3EB
Tel: (01437) 781254

Comfortable, modern house situated in peaceful countryside with a small nature reserve close by. An ideal location for visiting Pembrokeshire's many beautiful sandy bays, for sailing, surfing, walking the coastal paths or visiting the bird islands. Twin and double rooms available, one en-suite. Tea trays in bedrooms, spacious lounge/dining room. Colour television.

	SINGLE PER PERSON B&B	DOUBLE FOR 2 PERSONS B&B	🛏 2 / 🛁 1
MIN £	MAX £	MIN £	MAX £	OPEN
15.00	15.00	27.00	30.00	4-10

H	The Hope & Anchor Inn

Goodwick
SA64 0BP
Tel: (01348) 872314

Small family run Inn overlooking Fishguard Bay. Two minutes Sealink ferry. Restaurant, fresh sea food. All en-suite rooms. TV's, parking. On Coastal Path. Special diets. Dogs by arrangement. Vegetarian. Ramblers Guide, Cycle Touring Club, Les Routiers. Located end of A40.

	SINGLE PER PERSON B&B	DOUBLE FOR 2 PERSONS B&B	🛏 3 / 🛁 3
MIN £	MAX £	MIN £	MAX £	OPEN
-	20.00	-	36.00	1-12

GH	Seahorses

Freshwater East, **COMMENDED**
Pembroke
SA71 5LA
Tel: (01646) 672405

A welcoming comfortable guest house. Ideal touring centre within Pembrokeshire Coast National Park and close to coastal path, castles nearby. The many sandy beaches are within easy reach. Good food and friendly service. All bedrooms have H&C. TV lounge. Parking.

	SINGLE PER PERSON B&B	DOUBLE FOR 2 PERSONS B&B	🛏 - / 🛁 -
MIN £	MAX £	MIN £	MAX £	OPEN
-	-	28.00	30.00	5-9

GH	Glenfield

5 Atlantic Drive, L
Broad Haven,
Haverfordwest SA62 3JA
Tel: (01437) 781502

A warm welcome awaits you at my comfortable guest house with ample home cooked meals and friendly service. Hot and cold, tea making facilities in all rooms, full central heating, colour television, own key. 300 yards to beach and Coastal Path.

	SINGLE PER PERSON B&B	DOUBLE FOR 2 PERSONS B&B	🛏 4 / 🛁 -
MIN £	MAX £	MIN £	MAX £	OPEN
13.00	13.00	26.00	26.00	3-9

GH	Glanmoy Lodge (Private Suite)

Tref-Wrgi Road, **HIGHLY COMMENDED**
Goodwick.
Fishguard SA64 0JX
Tel: (01348) 874333
Fax: (01348) 874333

Totally private accommodation in our guest suite. Privacy and security guaranteed. No other guests to disturb you. Choice of double, twin, family accommodation with en-suite facilities. All rooms have alarm radio and TV. Telephones available. Choice of breakfast. Beautiful gardens and views. Very quiet. Ferry, beaches and town 1 mile. Late night travellers welcome.

	SINGLE PER PERSON B&B	DOUBLE FOR 2 PERSONS B&B	🛏 2 / 🛁 2
MIN £	MAX £	MIN £	MAX £	OPEN
20.00	20.00	28.00	36.00	1-12

FH	East Trewent Farm

Freshwater East,
Pembroke
SA71 5LR
Tel: (01646) 672127

Birds, flowers, fresh air in abundance. East Trewent farm adjoins the Coastal Path. Beach 400 yards. Fishing and riding nearby. Ideal for those who love the outdoor life. In the evening relax in the bar and enjoy the excellent cuisine in the Chough Restaurant. Open all year round.

	SINGLE PER PERSON B&B	DOUBLE FOR 2 PERSONS B&B	🛏 5 / 🛁 2
MIN £	MAX £	MIN £	MAX £	OPEN
15.50	19.00	31.00	38.00	1-12

FH	Trearched Farm Guest House

Croes-goch, **HIGHLY COMMENDED**
Haverfordwest,
SA62 3JP
Tel: (01348) 831310

Enjoy a relaxing break in our 18th century listed farmhouse on arable farm. Long drive entrance by Y Lodge on A487 in village. Sorry no dogs. Spacious grounds with small lake. Footpath link to coast at Tre-fin approximately 2.25 miles. Ideal walking and bird watching. Double, twin or single rooms. Self catering for two also available.

	SINGLE PER PERSON B&B	DOUBLE FOR 2 PERSONS B&B	🛏 6 / 🛁 -
MIN £	MAX £	MIN £	MAX £	OPEN
15.00	16.00	30.00	32.00	1-12

GH	Heathfield

Mathry Road, **HIGHLY COMMENDED**
Letterston
SA62 5EG
Tel: (01348) 840263

Our Georgian country house in its tranquil setting of pastures and woodlands is the perfect place to relax and be spoilt. It is ideally situated to explore Pembrokeshire's treasures. Comfortable guest rooms with beautiful views over rolling countryside, good food and wines. Scenic coastal walks, fishing, horseriding nearby. Golf only 1 mile away.

	SINGLE PER PERSON B&B	DOUBLE FOR 2 PERSONS B&B	🛏 3 / 🛁 3
MIN £	MAX £	MIN £	MAX £	OPEN
-	20.00	33.00	36.00	4-10

GH	The Fold

Cleddau Lodge,
Camrose,
Haverfordwest SA62 6HY
Tel: (01437) 710640

Converted 15th century farmhouse in secluded garden overlooking River Cleddau. Private fishing available. Central to Pembrokeshire Coast, 6 miles. Double bedroom, hot and cold water, TV, tea/coffee, own shower, toilet, separate entrance. Homely welcome, as one of the family. Part of 50 acre estate with gardens, woodlands and river. View of the Preseli Hills.

	SINGLE PER PERSON B&B	DOUBLE FOR 2 PERSONS B&B	🛏 1 / 🛁 0
MIN £	MAX £	MIN £	MAX £	OPEN
15.00	15.00	26.00	30.00	3-10

Haverfordwest Kilgetty Little Haven Llanfyrnach Maenclochog Newport

---

GH Greenways Guest House

Shoals Hook Lane,
Haverfordwest
SA61 2XN
Tel: (01437) 762345

HIGHLY COMMENDED

Set in two acres, picturesque gardens, picnic area, sun terrace, overlooking golf course, Preseli Mountains. Greenways is an ideal touring base. We are twenty minutes' drive from ferry terminals. Relax in comfort. All bedrooms are ground floor with en-suite facilities, service tray, hairdryer and colour TV. Private parking. A quiet retreat home from home. Children, pets welcome.

		SINGLE PER PERSON B&B		DOUBLE FOR 2 PERSONS B&B			3
		MIN £	MAX £	MIN £	MAX £	OPEN	3
		18.00	20.00	36.00	40.00	1-12	

FH Market Gate

Cresselly,
Kilgetty
SA68 0SH
Tel: (01646) 651684

COMMENDED
L

Situated near the beaches of Tenby and Saundersfoot, deep in the South Pembrokeshire countryside. Comfortable, traditional farmhouse on working family run farm in a peaceful location. Traditional home cooking where vegetarians and special diets are catered for. Children welcome. Large garden area. Colour TV, tea/coffee facilities and central heating in all rooms.

		SINGLE PER PERSON B&B		DOUBLE FOR 2 PERSONS B&B			3
		MIN £	MAX £	MIN £	MAX £	OPEN	-
		13.00	14.00	26.00	28.00	4-10	

FH Trepant Farm

Morvil, Rosebush,
Near Maenclochog
SA66 7RE
Tel: (01437) 532491

HIGHLY COMMENDED

Situated in the Pembrokeshire National Park, comfortable farmhouse in unspoilt countryside. A convenient base for many local activities, including superb walking and only 15 minutes from the coast with its abundance of wildlife and sandy beaches. 1 double en-suite, 1 twin bedroom. Good food is of prime importance, including vegetarian. Open April - October.

		SINGLE PER PERSON B&B		DOUBLE FOR 2 PERSONS B&B			2
		MIN £	MAX £	MIN £	MAX £	OPEN	1
		16.00	18.50	32.00	37.00	4-10	

FH Cuckoo Mill Farm

Pelcomb Bridge,
St David's Road,
Haverfordwest SA62 6EA
Tel: (01437) 762139

Ideally situated peacefully in central Pembrokeshire on working family farm. Two miles from Haverfordwest, ten minutes drive to coastline walks, sandy beaches, golf course, riding stables. Real home comfort in pretty heated rooms, H&C, tea trays, radio. Good home cooked meals of local produce. Evening meal. Personal attention. Reductions for senior citizens and children.

		SINGLE PER PERSON B&B		DOUBLE FOR 2 PERSONS B&B			3
		MIN £	MAX £	MIN £	MAX £	OPEN	1
		14.50	17.50	29.00	35.00	1-12	

GH Whitegates

Little Haven,
Haverfordwest
SA62 3LA
Tel: (01437) 781552

COMMENDED

Country house style accommodation overlooking St Brides Bay and fishing village with several good eating places. Ideal bird watching, wind surfing, or beach holidays. Warm welcome awaits you in this family home, with heated outdoor pool in season.

		SINGLE PER PERSON B&B		DOUBLE FOR 2 PERSONS B&B			3
		MIN £	MAX £	MIN £	MAX £	OPEN	2
		-	-	37.00	-	1-12	

GH Grove Park Guest House

Pen-y-Bont,
Newport
SA42 0LT
Tel: (01239) 820122

HIGHLY COMMENDED

Grove Park is situated on the outskirts of Newport, 100 yards from Pembrokeshire Coastal Path. 19th century house which has been completely refurbished, but retains original character. Estuary and mountain views, easy distance from large sandy beach and Preseli Mountains. Imaginative four course dinner menu. Winter breaks, log fires, hearty casseroles. Colour TV all bedrooms.

		SINGLE PER PERSON B&B		DOUBLE FOR 2 PERSONS B&B			4
		MIN £	MAX £	MIN £	MAX £	OPEN	2
		20.00	-	36.00	40.00	1-12	

FH Knock Farm

Camrose,
Haverfordwest
SA62 6NW
Tel: (01437) 762208

Our working dairy farm is peacefully situated in a scenic valley in central Pembrokeshire. Ten minutes from Pembrokeshire's sandy beaches and coastline walks, two miles from Haverfordwest. Ideally situated for fishing, horse riding, walking, golf. Tasty home cooking and homely atmosphere. Pretty C/H bedrooms. Tea/coffee facilities, large family room en-suite. Reductions children and senior citizens.

		SINGLE PER PERSON B&B		DOUBLE FOR 2 PERSONS B&B			3
		MIN £	MAX £	MIN £	MAX £	OPEN	1
		14.50	17.50	29.00	35.00	1-11	

FH Bron-y-Gaer

Llanfyrnach
SA35 0DA
Tel: (01239) 831265

Our peaceful smallholding, just three miles off the A478 near Crymych, offers an ideal touring base for exploring West Wales. Accommodation is in pretty en-suite bedrooms, all with tea/coffee making facilities. Guests have their own lounge with colour TV. We have a craftshop, hand spun garments, beautiful gardens and friendly farm animals.

		SINGLE PER PERSON B&B		DOUBLE FOR 2 PERSONS B&B			2
		MIN £	MAX £	MIN £	MAX £	OPEN	2
		16.00	16.00	32.00	32.00	1-12	

GH Springhill

Parrog Road,
Newport
SA42 0RH
Tel: (01239) 820626

A listed family house with a warm welcome. All rooms have wash basins, tea/coffee facilities, heaters, some with sea views. Ideally situated for walking the Pembrokeshire Coastal Path, Preseli Hills. Riding nearby. Evening meals and packed lunches by arrangement. Also available, a self catering apartment.

		SINGLE PER PERSON B&B		DOUBLE FOR 2 PERSONS B&B			3
		MIN £	MAX £	MIN £	MAX £	OPEN	
		14.50	-	29.00	-	1-12	

GH | Merton Place House

3 East Back,
Pembroke
SA71 4HL
Tel: (01646) 684796

APPROVED
L

Period town house with walled garden. French spoken. Only six guests taken. Basins, shaving points, tea/coffee facilities in all rooms. Private sitting room for visitors with TV, full of books. Vegetarian, French or English breakfast offered. Quiet position just off main street, convenient trains, buses, shops, restaurants and church. Full central heating. Sorry no pets. *i*

🛏, ✂	SINGLE PER PERSON B&B	DOUBLE FOR 2 PERSONS B&B	🛏 4
			🛁 -
	MIN £	MAX £	MIN £	MAX £	OPEN
	14.00	15.00	28.00	30.00	1-12

GH | Llainpropert Cottage

Treffynnon,
Croes-goch,
Haverfordwest
SA62 5JY
Tel: (01348) 831135

HIGHLY COMMENDED
L

A comfortable 200 year old cottage recently modernised, which is situated in attractive country but close to St David's, Fishguard and the wonderful Pembrokeshire coastline. All bedrooms have hot and hold and tea/coffee making facilities, one being en-suite. There is an attractive dining room and lounge, pleasant gardens, fields with Angora goats and ample car parking. *i*

P 🛏	SINGLE PER PERSON B&B	DOUBLE FOR 2 PERSONS B&B	🛏 3
🚫✗			🛁 1
	MIN £	MAX £	MIN £	MAX £	OPEN
	15.00	20.00	30.00	40.00	4-10

GH | Y-Gorlan Guest House

77 Nun Street,
St David's
Haverfordwest
SA62 6NU
Tel: (01437) 720837
Fax: (01437) 720837

HIGHLY COMMENDED

Family run guest house close to cathedral, local attractions, beach, golf course, coastal paths. All rooms en-suite, guest lounge with panoramic views, licensed, restaurant. RAC Acclaimed. Discounts for children under 10 years. Book 7 nights, pay for 6. Open all year. *i*

P 🍴	SINGLE PER PERSON B&B	DOUBLE FOR 2 PERSONS B&B	🛏 5
🛏, 🍽			🛁 5
	MIN £	MAX £	MIN £	MAX £	OPEN
	18.50	20.00	35.00	39.00	1-12

FH | Bangeston Farm

Stackpole,
Pembroke
SA71 5BX
Tel: (01646) 683986

Homely farmhouse on working farm in peaceful countryside with views of Stackpole and St Govan's Head. Three miles from Pembroke, good walking area and a base from which to explore the Pembrokeshire Coast National Park. Early reservations are advised. Home cooked hearty breakfasts. Tea/coffee making facilities, hot and cold in bedrooms. Colour TV in lounge. Cots and highchairs available. Brochure from Mrs Mathias. *i*

P 🛏	SINGLE PER PERSON B&B	DOUBLE FOR 2 PERSONS B&B	🛏 3
			🛁 -
	MIN £	MAX £	MIN £	MAX £	OPEN
	12.50	15.00	25.00	30.00	4-9

GH | Tŷ Olaf

Mount Gardens,
St David's
SA62 6BS
Tel: (01437) 720885
Fax: (01437) 720885

HIGHLY COMMENDED
L

Quiet family home on edge of Britain's smallest cathedral city in Pembrokeshire Coast National Park. Double, twin, single and family rooms. Central heating, H&C, shaver points, tea/coffee, TV lounge, no stairs. Off - road parking. Five minute's walk to cathedral and good restaurants. Convenient for Coast Path, boat trips, beaches etc. *i*

P 🛏	SINGLE PER PERSON B&B	DOUBLE FOR 2 PERSONS B&B	🛏 4
🚫✗			🛁 -
	MIN £	MAX £	MIN £	MAX £	OPEN
	13.50	15.50	27.00	31.00	4-10

GH | The Ark

St Florence,
Near Tenby
SA70 8LN
Tel: (01834) 871654

HIGHLY COMMENDED

Small Pembrokeshire cottage, situated in the floral village of St. Florance, which has been totally refurbished to a very high standard. Provides Highly Commended and highly recommended B&B accommodation for non smoking guests, who will appreciate the quiet village location. All the en-suite bedrooms are equipped with colour TV and well stocked beverage tray. Central heating. *i*

P 🛏	SINGLE PER PERSON B&B	DOUBLE FOR 2 PERSONS B&B	🛏 3
🚫✗			🛁 3
	MIN £	MAX £	MIN £	MAX £	OPEN
	-	-	33.00	-	2-11

GH | Awel-Môr Guest House

Penparc, Tre-fin,
Near St David's
SA62 5AG
Tel: (01348) 837865
Fax: (01348) 837865

DE LUXE

Luxury "non smoking" accommodation. Magnificent views overlooking sea and Pembrokeshire National Park. Large bedrooms with CH, soft chairs, TV, tea/coffee facilities. Delicious food from breakfast/ dinner menu. Optional evening meal. "Taste of Wales" member. Table licence. Free brochure available. "Best Guest House in Wales", Wales Tourist Board Hospitality Award. Map grid ref. SM845312. *i*

P 🍴	SINGLE PER PERSON B&B	DOUBLE FOR 2 PERSONS B&B	🛏 3
🛏, 🍽			🛁 2
	MIN £	MAX £	MIN £	MAX £	OPEN
	18.00	-	36.00	-	4-10

GH | Y Glennydd Restaurant & Guest House

51 Nun Street,
St David's
SA62 6NU
Tel: (01437) 720576
Fax: (01437) 720184

COMMENDED

A comfortable Victorian house with 10 spacious centrally heated rooms, all with H&C, teasmade, colour TV, many with splendid views, most rooms with en-suite facilities. We also offer a licensed restaurant, an elegant lounge and friendly service. Ideal centre for walking, bird watching and outdoor activities. *i*

c 🍴	SINGLE PER PERSON B&B	DOUBLE FOR 2 PERSONS B&B	🛏 10
🛏, ✂ 🍽			🛁 7
	MIN £	MAX £	MIN £	MAX £	OPEN
	15.00	20.00	30.00	38.00	2-10

GH | Flemish Court

St Florence,
Tenby
SA70 8LS
Tel: (01834) 871413

COMMENDED

Lovely home of June and Eric where you will find a real Welsh welcome. All rooms en-suite. Sumptuous breakfast. All day access. Situated in the floral village. Norman church opposite. Easy access to all attractions, coastal walks etc. Try us first for that restful relaxing holiday you all deserve. Evening meals available. Telephone June Taylor for brochure. Safe parking. *i*

P 🛏	SINGLE PER PERSON B&B	DOUBLE FOR 2 PERSONS B&B	🛏 3
🛏, ✂ 🍽			🛁 3
	MIN £	MAX £	MIN £	MAX £	OPEN
	15.00	17.00	30.00	33.00	1-12

St Ishmael's Saundersfoot Solva Tenby

FH | **Skerryback**

Sandy Haven,
St Ishmaels
SA62 3DN
Tel: (01646) 636598

 HIGHLY COMMENDED

A warm Welsh welcome in a Pembrokeshire farmhouse on the Coastal Footpath. A walkers' sanctuary. Ideal for visiting Skomer and Skokholm and exploring Pembrokeshire's beautiful coastline. All home comforts with open fires in winter, tea/coffee facilities etc.

i

		SINGLE PER PERSON B&B		DOUBLE FOR 2 PERSONS B&B		🛏 2
P	🍴					-
MIN £ 15.00	MAX £ 16.00	MIN £ 15.00	MAX £ 16.00		OPEN 1-12	

GH | **Pinewood**

Wiseman's Bridge,
Saundersfoot,
Narberth SA67 8NU
Tel: (01834) 811082

 HIGHLY COMMENDED

Enjoy a peaceful relaxing holiday in our comfortable home in rural surroundings, halfway between Saundersfoot and Amroth, alongside the coastal path; 350 yards from beach and inn. Twin and double rooms are en-suite with colour TV, and tea/coffee facilities, two are ground floor. Lounge has sea views. Ideal for beaches, sightseeing and walking.

i

		SINGLE PER PERSON B&B		DOUBLE FOR 2 PERSONS B&B		🛏 3
P						3
MIN £ 14.00	MAX £ 16.00	MIN £ 28.00	MAX £ 32.00		OPEN 1-12	

FH | **Llanddinog Old Farmhouse**

Solva,
Haverfordwest
SA62 6NA
Tel: (01348) 831224

Peaceful 16th century farmhouse, situated only 3 miles from sandy beaches and coastal paths. Excellent facilities include roaring fires. Substantial country food using local ingredients. Children enjoy the large garden, rope swings, aerial slide, small animals. Riding, golf, mountain bikes nearby. picnics prepared. Pets welcome. Close to Solva Harbour, St David's Cathedral, castles, Preseli Mountains. SAE please, Mrs S Griffiths.

i

		SINGLE PER PERSON B&B		DOUBLE FOR 2 PERSONS B&B		🛏 2
P						2
		MIN £ 20.00	MAX £ -	MIN £ 32.00	MAX £ -	OPEN 1-12

H | **Cliff House**

Wogan Terrace,
Saundersfoot
SA69 9HA
Tel: (01834) 813931

 HIGHLY COMMENDED

Quality, comfort, service, welcome - words our guests tell us really mean something at Cliff House. In the heart of the village, one minute from beach, with outstanding sea and harbour views. Ideal base for relaxation, sporting holidays or exploring beautiful Pembrokeshire. Quality en-suite facilities in several rooms (supplement payable). Personal service from resident proprietors.

i

		SINGLE PER PERSON B&B		DOUBLE FOR 2 PERSONS B&B		🛏 6
						3
MIN £ -	MAX £ -	MIN £ 32.00	MAX £ 38.00		OPEN 1-12	

FH | **Carne Mountain Farm**

Reynalton,
Kilgetty
SA68 0PD
Tel: (01834) 860546

 COMMENDED L

A warm welcome awaits you at our 200 year old farmhouse. Set amidst the peace and tranquility of the beautiful Pembrokeshire countryside. Distant views of Preseli Hills, yet only 3.5 miles from Saundersfoot. Picturesque bedrooms with TV, tea/coffee, wash hand basins, central heating. Separate dining room with interesting plate collection. Delicious farmhouse food. SAE Mrs Joy Holgate.

i

		SINGLE PER PERSON B&B		DOUBLE FOR 2 PERSONS B&B		🛏 2
P						-
MIN £ 13.50	MAX £ 14.50	MIN £ 27.00	MAX £ 29.00		OPEN 1-12	

H | **Clarence House Hotel**

Esplanade,
Tenby SA70 7DU
Tel: (01834) 844371
Fax: (01834) 844372

 COMMENDED

Tenby town centre esplanade. South Beach sea front.

Send for free colour brochure. Full information, discount tariff options. All you need to know.

i

		SINGLE PER PERSON B&B		DOUBLE FOR 2 PERSONS B&B		🛏 29
						29
MIN £ 13.00	MAX £ 20.00	MIN £ 20.00	MAX £ 40.00		OPEN 4-9	

H | **The Grange Hotel**

Wooden,
Saundersfoot
SA69 9DY
Tel: (01834) 812809
Fax: (01834) 812809

 COMMENDED

Comfortable, family run, licensed hotel close to Saundersfoot, Tenby and the Pembrokeshire Coastal Path. All rooms have tea/coffee, colour TV and central heating. There is a large car park. An ideal base for beach and watersports holidays, bird watching, walking and fishing. Reductions are available for weekly bookings and children. Brochure: Mrs Shelagh Griffin - Proprietor.

		SINGLE PER PERSON B&B		DOUBLE FOR 2 PERSONS B&B		🛏 6
P						2
MIN £ -	MAX £ -	MIN £ 28.00	MAX £ 40.00		OPEN 4-10	

H | **The Cottage Court Hotel**

Narberth Road,
Tenby
SA70 8HT
Tel: (01834) 843650

COMMENDED

The hotel stands in its own grounds in a a quiet part of Tenby, away from the bustle of the town but within a few minutes' walk of the beaches and town centre. Ample car parking in hotel grounds. Excellent cuisine and hospitality. For further details telephone or write for brochure.

i

		SINGLE PER PERSON B&B		DOUBLE FOR 2 PERSONS B&B		🛏 12
P	C					10
		MIN £ 17.50	MAX £ 20.00	MIN £ 17.50	MAX £ 20.00	OPEN 3-11

Tenby

H	Hammonds Park Hotel

Narberth Road,
Tenby SA70 8HT
Tel: (01834) 842696
Fax: (01834) 842696

 COMMENDED

New Zealand cooking, Welsh hospitality. The hotel is situated within its own gardens, with car parking for all guests. All rooms are en-suite with TV's, direct dial telephone, beverages, CH, some 4 posters; some ground floor. Discounts for senior citizens and children (cot/highchairs available). Special short breaks. AA*. Phone, fax or Email COMPUSERVE 100445,101.

		SINGLE PER PERSON B&B	DOUBLE FOR 2 PERSONS B&B	🛏 10
P 🐾 ⛾ 🏠 ✂ 🍴				🛏 10
		MIN £ 15.00	MAX £ 20.00	MIN £ 30.00	MAX £ 40.00	OPEN 1-12

GH	High Seas

8 The Norton,
Tenby
SA70 8AA
Tel: (01834) 843611/842491
Fax: (01834) 843611

COMMENDED

This Georgian town house is in an ideal position with beautiful views of the beach and harbour. Close to town centre and only a few steps from the sands and safe bathing of the North Beach. There are six bedrooms, five with private bathroom. All rooms have colour TV and tea making facilities.

	SINGLE PER PERSON B&B	DOUBLE FOR 2 PERSONS B&B	🛏 6
🏠			🛏 5
	MIN £ 14.00	MAX £ 19.00	MIN £ 28.00	MAX £ 39.00	OPEN 4-10

GH	Sutherlands

3 Picton Road,
Tenby
SA70 7DP
Tel: (01834) 842522

👑

Small family run guest house, ideally situated for all the delights of the attractive walled town. Golf links, bowling green and beautiful unspoilt beaches, all within easy reach. Noted for our hospitality and "rich" breakfasts. The discerning palate will also appreciate our evening meals.

		SINGLE PER PERSON B&B	DOUBLE FOR 2 PERSONS B&B	🛏 3
✂ 🍴				🛏 1
		MIN £ 14.00	MAX £ 18.00	MIN £ 28.00	MAX £ 36.00	OPEN 1-12

Tenby harbour

67

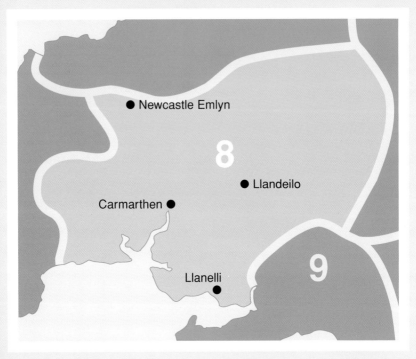

Dylan Thomas captured the essence of this timeless part of Wales in his short stories and poems, but most of all in his masterwork, *Under Milk Wood*. Dylan lived at Laugharne, a sleepy seatown set amongst the sweeping sands of Carmarthen Bay. Here you can wander along endless beaches, and then turn your attention to the patchwork of green farmlands which roll gently down to the sea. There's a rare sense of peace and tranquillity in the countryside around Carmarthen. Explore the lovely Vale of Towy, the moors of Mynydd Llanybydder or the glades of the Brechfa Forest. And don't miss market day at Carmarthen, or the view from the ramparts of Carreg Cennen, one of Wales's most spectacular castles.

It's a fact...

In the 1920s, the huge 6-mile beach at Pendine was used for land speed record attempts. Dolaucothi, Pumsaint, is the only place in Britain where we know, for certain, that the Romans mined for gold. The beach at Cefn Sidan, Pembrey, is 7 miles long. Twm Shôn Cati, Wales's answer to Robin Hood, hid in the hills north of Llandovery from the Sheriff of Carmarthen. Christmas mail can be postmarked from Bethlehem, a hamlet between Llandeilo and Llangadog.

Fe6   Abergorlech

Village tucked away in Cothi Valley, flanked by green farmlands and the Brechfa Forest. Tranquil fishing and walking country. Beautiful lakeside ruins of Talley Abbey nearby

Ke2   Ammanford

Bustling valley town, good for Welsh crafts and products, on western edge of Brecon Beacons National Park. Spectacular mountain routes over nearby Black Mountain to Llangadog.

Kc2   Carmarthen

Prosperous country town in pastoral Vale of Towy. Lively market and shops, livestock market. Carmarthen Castle was an important residence of the native Welsh princes but only the gateway and towers remain. Golf, fishing, tennis and well-equipped leisure centre. Remains of Roman amphitheatre. Immaculate museum in beautiful historic house on outskirts of town. Gwili Railway and ornamental Middleton Hall Amenity Area nearby.

Kc3   Kidwelly

Historic town 9 miles south of Carmarthen. Its first charter was granted by Henry I. With its ancient church, 14th-century bridge and great castle – one of the best preserved in Wales – it has a medieval air. Interesting little museum near castle. Industrial museum on outskirts. Located on Gwendraeth Estuary, the town is close to Cefn Sidan Sands and Pembrey Country Park.

Ga7   Llandeilo

Farming centre at an important crossing on River Towy, and handy as touring base for Carreg Cennen Castle, impressively set on high crag, and remains of Dryslwyn Castle. Limited access to Dinefwr Castle in magnificent parklands on edge of town. Gelli Aur Country Park nearby has 36 hectares/90 acres, including a nature trail, arboretum and deer herd.

Gb6   Llandovery

An important market town on the A40 with a ruined castle; its Welsh name Llanymddyfri means 'the church among the waters'. In the hills to the north is the cave of Twm Siôn Cati – theWelsh Robin Hood. Good touring centre for Brecon Beacons and remote Llyn Brianne area.

Kd4   Llanelli

Bustling town with good shopping, covered market and pleasant parklands. Wildfowl and Wetlands Centre on estuary modelled on Slimbridge. Pembrey Country Park, adjoining 7 miles of sandy beach, has a visitor centre and many attractions including pony trekking, ski slope, adventure playground. The Welsh Motor Sports Centre and Kidwelly Castle and Industrial Museum are nearby.

Fb6   Newcastle Emlyn

Market town on the River Teifi surrounded by rolling farmland and noted for its fine fishing. The Teifi Valley Railway and Museum of the Welsh Woollen Industry are nearby attractions. A good base for touring north Pembrokeshire and Teifi Valley. You may see coracle fishing at nearby Cenarth where the old mill is open to visitors.

Cefn Sidan Sands, Pembrey

Abergorlech Ammanford Carmarthen Kidwelly

GH | **Gorlech House**

Abergorlech,
Near Carmarthen
SA32 7SJ
Tel: (01558) 685211

COMMENDED
L

We are a large comfortable house with our own spacious garden, located in the award winning village of Abergorlech. Situated at the edge of the beautiful Brechfa Forest. We are ideal for interesting forest walks. Exciting salmon fishing. We have mountain bikes available for our guests. We offer a most relaxing enjoyable country holiday.

		SINGLE PER PERSON B&B		DOUBLE FOR 2 PERSONS B&B		🛏 2 🛁
P ✕ 🍴	🏠	MIN £	MAX £	MIN £	MAX £	OPEN
		-	-	30.00	30.00	3-11

GH | **Old Priory Guest House**

20 Priory Street,
Carmarthen
SA31 1NE
Tel: (01267) 237471

L

Family run guest house situated five minutes from town centre; bus and train station within walking distance. A la carte restaurant and bar. Televisions in all bedrooms, centrally heated throughout. Fifteen bedrooms, all with views of the Towy Valley.

		SINGLE PER PERSON B&B		DOUBLE FOR 2 PERSONS B&B		🛏 15 🛁 -
🍴 🏠		MIN £	MAX £	MIN £	MAX £	OPEN
		17.50	20.00	29.00	34.00	1-12

FH | **Trebersed Farmhouse**

Travellers Rest,
St Peters
Carmarthen SA31 3RR
Tel: (01267) 238182
Fax: (01267) 223633

HIGHLY COMMENDED

A warm welcome awaits you at our working dairy farm overlooking the thriving market town of Carmarthen. Only two miles from its centre, plenty of parking space. Excellent touring base, 0.75 miles off A40. Three comfortable rooms, all en-suite, tea/coffee, central heating, radio alarms. Colour TV lounge. Enquiries or brochure Mrs Rosemary Jones.

		SINGLE PER PERSON B&B		DOUBLE FOR 2 PERSONS B&B		🛏 3 🛁 3
P 🏠 ✕	🐕	MIN £	MAX £	MIN £	MAX £	OPEN
		18.00	20.00	34.00	34.00	1-12

GH | **Mount Pleasant**

Pontardulais Road,
Garnswllt,
Ammanford SA18 2RT
Tel: (01269) 591722
Fax: (01269) 591722

COMMENDED
L

Enjoy the best of both worlds. Relax in peaceful surroundings with magnificent views over Loughor Valley and the convenient location. 2.5 miles from Ammanford market town and 5 miles from M4 motorway. In easy reach of Swansea shopping and leisure facilities and many tourist attractions. A warm welcome awaits you.

		SINGLE PER PERSON B&B		DOUBLE FOR 2 PERSONS B&B		🛏 5 🛁 2
P 🐕 🏠 ✕ 🍴		MIN £	MAX £	MIN £	MAX £	OPEN
		16.00	18.00	28.00	32.00	1-12

GH | **Troedyrhiw Country Guest House**

Llanfynydd,
Carmarthen
SA32 7TQ
Tel: (01558) 668792

HIGHLY COMMENDED

Set in glorious countryside, this traditional Welsh farmhouse offers you a warm welcome with excellent food and luxurious accommodation. Enjoy strolling in 8 acres of grounds with Jacob sheep and a small vineyard. An ideal base for that relaxing holiday you've always promised yourself with castles, crafts and coast all near by, ready to be explored.

		SINGLE PER PERSON B&B		DOUBLE FOR 2 PERSONS B&B		🛏 3 🛁 3
P 🏠 ✕ 🍴		MIN £	MAX £	MIN £	MAX £	OPEN
		-	-	38.00	38.00	3-10

Wales Tourist Map

- **Our best-selling map – now with a new look**
- **Detailed 5 miles/inch scale**
- **Wealth of tourist information**
- **14 specially devised car tours**
- **Town plans**

£2 inc. p&p (see 'Get Yourself a Guide' at the end of the book)

GH | **Glasfryn Guest House and Restaurant**

Brechfa,
Carmarthen
SA32 7QY
Tel: (01267) 202306

HIGHLY COMMENDED

Situated at the edge of Brechfa Forest, a small family owned guest house. Ideally located for walking, pony trekking, bird watching, mountain bike trails. All rooms en-suite, excellent home cooking, licensed restaurant. 20 minutes from Carmarthen, 45 minutes Blue Flag beach. 1.25 hours Fishguard ferry. "Taste of Wales" member.

		SINGLE PER PERSON B&B		DOUBLE FOR 2 PERSONS B&B		🛏 3 🛁 3
P 🏠 🍴	🐕	MIN £	MAX £	MIN £	MAX £	OPEN
		-	-	40.00	40.00	1-12

FH | **Plas Farmhouse**

Llangynog,
Carmarthen
SA38 5DB
Tel: (01267) 211492

Spacious farmhouse situated five miles west of Carmarthen, just off A40 in quiet location. Ideal base for touring. Twin, double, family rooms all with tea/coffee making facilities and TV. En-suite rooms available. One hour's drive from the Fishguard/Pembroke ferries to Ireland. Good evening meals available at local inn. Special mid week breaks available.

		SINGLE PER PERSON B&B		DOUBLE FOR 2 PERSONS B&B		🛏 3 🛁 2
P 🏠 ✕	🐕	MIN £	MAX £	MIN £	MAX £	OPEN
		16.00	20.00	30.00	34.00	1-12

FH | **Penlan Isaf Farm**

Kidwelly
SA17 5JR
Tel: (01554) 890084
Fax: (01554) 891191

DE LUXE

Penlan Isaf overlooks the historic town of Kidwelly with superb views of the countryside and Gower coast. Pembrey Park and Motor Centre two miles. Penlan is a 250 acre dairy farm with modern comfortable farmhouse. En-suite, colour TV all bedrooms. Sunlounge. A warm welcome and excellent home cooking awaits visitors; children are welcome at the farm.

		SINGLE PER PERSON B&B		DOUBLE FOR 2 PERSONS B&B		🛏 3 🛁 3
P 🏠 🍴	🐕 ✕	MIN £	MAX £	MIN £	MAX £	OPEN
		18.00	20.00	32.00	35.00	1-12

GH | Tŷ Cefn Tregib

Ffairfach,
Llandeilo
SA19 6TD
Tel: (01558) 823942

HIGHLY COMMENDED

Converted 18th century stone barn, oak timbered, light and airy. Provides quiet, comfortable accommodation. Private wooded setting with open country views. 10 minutes' walk village, pubs, swimming pool, BR. 1 double, 1 en-suite twin, both with colour tv, tea/coffee, separate lounge, use of garden. A peaceful, friendly yet convenient base for touring, exploring or just relaxing.

		SINGLE PER PERSON B&B		DOUBLE FOR 2 PERSONS B&B			2
		MIN £	MAX £	MIN £	MAX £	OPEN	1
		-	-	30.00	35.00	1-12	

GH | Pen-y-Bont

Llangadog
SA19 9EN
Tel: (01550) 777126

HIGHLY COMMENDED

Charming country house in tranquil streamside setting, fringe Brecon Beacons National Park. Pretty bedrooms with own bathrooms. Comfortable lounge, separate dining room. Emphasis on good service and excellent food, with fresh produce. Beautiful gardens. Car park. Ideally placed for exploring this lovely country. Abundant wildlife and a bird watcher's paradise. Home of the red kite.

		SINGLE PER PERSON B&B		DOUBLE FOR 2 PERSONS B&B			3
		MIN £	MAX £	MIN £	MAX £	OPEN	3
		17.00	17.00	34.00	34.00	1-12	

H | The Stepney Hotel

Park Street,
Llanelli SA15 3YE
Tel: (01554) 752112
Fax: (01550) 751428

Once an 18th century coaching inn this family run hotel, situated in the town centre, prides itself on giving excellent value for money. 34 bedrooms, many en-suite, free parking, olde worlde bar and restaurant serving imaginative food. A guaranteed friendly and warm welcome to all. B&B from £16.50, children welcome.

		SINGLE PER PERSON B&B		DOUBLE FOR 2 PERSONS B&B			33
		MIN £	MAX £	MIN £	MAX £	OPEN	12
		19.50	19.50	33.00	33.00	1-12	

GH | Myrtle Hill Guest House

Llansadwrn,
Llanwrda
SA19 8HL
Tel: (01550) 777530

COMMENDED

Old farmhouse with magnificent views in unspoilt countryside. All bedrooms with en-suite bathrooms, tea/coffee facilities. Two sitting rooms, one "no smoking". Access at all times. Excellent food, freshly prepared using own garden produce. Ideally situated for exploring South, West and Mid Wales. Abundant wildlife, fishing, pony trekking, lovely walking country.

		SINGLE PER PERSON B&B		DOUBLE FOR 2 PERSONS B&B			3
		MIN £	MAX £	MIN £	MAX £	OPEN	3
		19.00	-	38.00	-	3-10	

FH | Cwmgwyn Farm

Llangadog Road,
Llandovery SA20 0EQ
Tel: (01550) 720410
Fax: (01550) 720262

HIGHLY COMMENDED

Warm welcome to enjoy the country on our livestock farm overlooking the River Towy, two miles from Llandovery on A4069. The 17th century farmhouse is full of charm and character with inglenook fireplace, exposed stonework and beams. Spacious luxury en-suite bedrooms with hairdryer, colour TV, tea/coffee. Ideally situated for touring Mid and South Wales.

		SINGLE PER PERSON B&B		DOUBLE FOR 2 PERSONS B&B			3
		MIN £	MAX £	MIN £	MAX £	OPEN	3
		19.00	20.00	38.00	40.00	4-10	

GH | Pensarn Guest House

Dre-fach Felindre,
Llandysul
SA44 5UQ
Tel: (01559) 371214

HIGHLY COMMENDED

Small and friendly non-smoking accommodation. Pretty house with garden, stream. One twin, one double. Private bathroom available. Tea/coffee making facilities and TV in rooms. Guests' own dining room and lounge with log fire. Lovely unspoilt countryside, ideal walking, driving. Beautiful coastline, crafts, museums, mills, castles, wildlife centres. Leaflet - Angela McDonald.

		SINGLE PER PERSON B&B		DOUBLE FOR 2 PERSONS B&B			2
		MIN £	MAX £	MIN £	MAX £	OPEN	1
		13.50	20.00	27.00	36.00	1-12	

Newcastle Emlyn

71

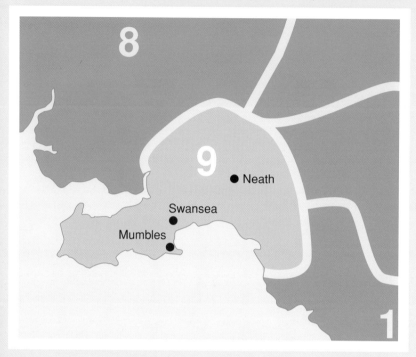

The city of Swansea enjoys a wonderful location. It stands on the grand curve of Swansea Bay at the doorstep to the beautiful Gower Peninsula and green Vale of Neath. It's a maritime city through and through – there's even a stylish Maritime Quarter complete with marina and attractive waterside developments. Modern and traditional Wales mix happily in this friendly city. At its heart is a fresh foods market where you can buy welshcakes, laverbread and cockles from Penclawdd on Gower. The pretty little sailing centre of Mumbles stands at the gateway to Gower, a lovely peninsula with a string of sandy, south-facing bays and a towering curtain of cliffs. Inland, there are the waterfalls and forests of the Vale of Neath to explore.

It's a fact...

In 1956, the Gower Peninsula was the first part of Britain to be declared an 'Area of Outstanding Natural Beauty'. Swansea Museum, Wales's oldest museum, dates from the 1830s. The inaugural meeting of the Welsh Rugby Union was held at Neath in 1881. The waterwheel at the National Trust's Aberdulais Falls is Europe's largest electricity-generating waterwheel. The traditional Welsh delicacy known as laverbread (a kind of puréed seaweed) is usually eaten as an accompaniment to bacon and eggs.

La4   Mumbles

Small resort on Swansea Bay with attractive waterfront and headland pier; centre for watersports and sailing. On fringe of Gower Peninsula, a designated 'Area of Outstanding Natural Beauty'. Oystermouth Castle and Clyne Valley Country Park and Gardens nearby.

Kd5   Oxwich

Popular Gower Peninsula beach with 3 miles of glorious sand and extensive dunes; easily accessible. Nature trail and visitor centre.

Ke5   Parkmill

Gower Peninsula village with easy access to beaches and Swansea. Visit Y Felin Ddŵr Craft and Countryside Centre. Three Cliffs Bay – one of the finest stretches of Gower – and historic sites nearby.

Kd5   Reynoldston

Gower Peninsula village near the sandy beaches of Oxwich, Port-Eynon and Rhosili.

Ke5   Southgate

Gower Peninsula village; fine beaches at Three Cliffs Bay and Oxwich, and popular Caswell and Langland bays just to the east. Close to Swansea with its leisure centre, Maritime Quarter, museums and shopping.

Langland Bay

Mumbles from Oystermouth Castle (top)

Mumbles Oxwich Parkmill Reynoldston Southgate

GH | The Coast House

708 Mumbles Road,
Mumbles, Swansea
SA3 4EH
Tel: (01792) 368702

HIGHLY COMMENDED

We are a well established family run guest house with a very high standard of accommodation. All our rooms have colour TV, tea-making, radio/alarms and hairdryers. Most rooms are en-suite. All rooms (except single en-suite) have sea views. We have received a Two Crown, Highly Commended rating, from the Wales Tourist Board.

i

		SINGLE PER PERSON B&B	DOUBLE FOR 2 PERSONS B&B	🛏 6 🛁 3
MIN £ 17.00	MAX £ 19.00	MIN £ 30.00	MAX £ 37.00	OPEN 1-12

FH | Parc-Le-Breos House

Parkmill,
Gower, Swansea
SA3 2HA
Tel: (01792) 371636

COMMENDED

Spacious 18th century farmhouse in the heart of the beautiful Gower Peninsula. Ideal base for a wide range of holiday activities around Gower. Riding holidays and day rides available, paddock rides for children. Home grown cooked food, warm welcome. BHS approved. AA Listed. SAE for colour brochure.

i

		SINGLE PER PERSON B&B	DOUBLE FOR 2 PERSONS B&B	🛏 10 🛁 8
MIN £ 16.00	MAX £ 18.00	MIN £ 16.00	MAX £ 18.00	OPEN 1-12

FH | Sunnyside Farm

Llanddewi Castle
Reynoldston,
Swansea SA3 1AU
Tel: (01792) 390194

L

Situated on Gower Peninsula, comfortable B&B accommodation with one family double and one twin bedroom on working farm. Guests welcome to look around. All home cooking, welcome tea/coffee on arrival, full central heating, evening meal optional. Children welcome at reduced rate. Enquiries to Jane James.

i

		SINGLE PER PERSON B&B	DOUBLE FOR 2 PERSONS B&B	🛏 2 🛁 -
MIN £ -	MAX £ 16.00	MIN £ -	MAX £ 32.00	OPEN 1-12

GH | Rock Villa

1 George Bank,
Southend, Mumbles,
Swansea SA3 4EQ
Tel: (01792) 366794

HIGHLY COMMENDED

Family run guest house. Easy access. Children's park/play area, tennis, bowls, sailing, skiing, wind surfing, fishing, cliff walks and beaches.

i

		SINGLE PER PERSON B&B	DOUBLE FOR 2 PERSONS B&B	🛏 6 🛁 3
MIN £ 16.00	MAX £ 20.00	MIN £ 32.00	MAX £ 36.00	OPEN 1-12

FH | Lunnon Farm

Parkmill,
Swansea
SA3 2EJ
Tel: (01792) 371205

L

Working dairy farm, 17th century, situated in superb position for Three Cliffs Bay, and within easy reach of all other Gower beaches. Lovely walks. All amenities in village of Parkmill. TV lounge, separate dining room, shower. Large bathroom. Hearty breakfasts. Pony trekking nearby. Within easy reach of Three Cliffs Bay, Swansea 8 miles. A warm Welsh welcome always.

i

		SINGLE PER PERSON B&B	DOUBLE FOR 2 PERSONS B&B	🛏 2 🛁 -
MIN £ -	MAX £ -	MIN £ 28.00	MAX £ 30.00	OPEN 3-10

GH | Little Haven Guest House

Oxwich,
Gower, Swansea
SA3 1LS
Tel: (01792) 390940

Family run guest house situated in Oxwich village. Located near beach, which is ideal for most water sports. Hot and cold water, tea and coffee making facilities in all bedrooms. En-suite family room available. Also, self catering bungalow available. No pets allowed in either property.

i

		SINGLE PER PERSON B&B	DOUBLE FOR 2 PERSONS B&B	🛏 3 🛁 1
MIN £ 17.00	MAX £ 19.00	MIN £ 34.00	MAX £ 34.00	OPEN 1-12

FH | Greenways Hills Farm

Reynoldston,
Gower, Swansea
SA3 1AE
Tel: (01792) 390125

L

This 120 acre working farm, in the beautiful village of Reynoldston, is adjacent to Cefn Bryn, a walker's paradise. Central to all Gower bays. Full central heating, H&C in bedrooms. Separate tables. TV lounge. Pets by arrangement. Car park. Bowling green, tennis courts and squash courts available within reasonable distance. Enquiries to D W John.

i

		SINGLE PER PERSON B&B	DOUBLE FOR 2 PERSONS B&B	🛏 3 🛁 3
MIN £ 16.00	MAX £ 18.00	MIN £ 28.00	MAX £ 32.00	OPEN 2-11

GH | Heatherlands

Southgate,
Gower,
Swansea SA3 2AP
Tel: (01792) 233256

HIGHLY COMMENDED

Delightfully situated Heatherlands is an immaculate residence. Secluded garden near cliff and sea. Short walk Pobbles and Three Cliffs Bay. Bedrooms with hot and cold, shaver points and tea making facilities. One bedroom with private bath. two bedrooms share shower room with toilet. TV lounge, separate tables in dining room. Excellent breakfasts. Parking. Warm welcome.

i

		SINGLE PER PERSON B&B	DOUBLE FOR 2 PERSONS B&B	🛏 3 🛁 1
MIN £ 18.00	MAX £ 19.00	MIN £ 34.00	MAX £ 36.00	OPEN 1-11

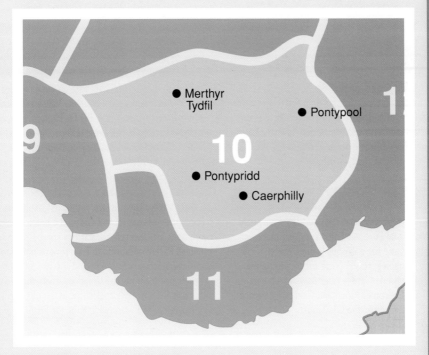

The Valleys of South Wales are full of surprises – dramatic natural beauty, country and wildlife parks, forest and cycle trails, and a huge range of attractions. Did you know that Caerphilly Castle is regarded as one of Europe's greatest surviving examples of medieval military architecture? Or that there's a scenic narrow-gauge railway which takes you into the foothills of the Brecon Beacons from Merthyr Tydfil? Or that you can enjoy everything from walking to watersports at an exceptional range of country parks? Yet the past hasn't been entirely forgotten. Although the Valleys are green again, there's a rich industrial heritage at places like the Big Pit Mining Museum, Blaenafon, and the Rhondda Heritage Park, Trehafod.

It's a fact...

Caerphilly Castle, which covers 12 hectares/30 acres, is one of Britain's largest. Its 'leaning tower' out-leans Pisa's. In the 19th century, Merthyr Tydfil was Wales's largest town and the 'iron capital of the world'. The world's first steam engine, built by Cornishman Richard Trevithick, ran from Merthyr to Abercynon in 1804. There are around 15 country parks in the Valleys. Pontypridd is singer Tom Jones's home town. Blaenafon's Big Pit Mining Museum was a working colliery until 1980. The last coalmine in the Rhondda closed at the end of 1990.

Mb3   Blackwood

Southern valley town surrounded by pine-clad hills rising to mountain tops. Visit Penyfan Pond, a country park a few miles to the north, attractive Parc Cwm Darran and the Sirhowy Valley Country Park. Tour Llancaiach Fawr historic house and Stuart Crystal's glass factory nearby.

Ma4   Caerphilly

A sight not to be missed – 13th-century Caerphilly Castle is one of Europe's finest surviving medieval strongholds and has a famous leaning tower. Golf course, shopping, good centre for exploring the Valleys and visiting Cardiff. Fine views and pleasant walks from Caerphilly Mountain. Caerphilly cheese made at the Old Court.

Mc3   Pontypool

Town with metal-producing past on eastern edge of South Wales Valleys. Park contains Valley Inheritance Centre and dry ski slope. Big Pit Mining Museum nearby, Llandegfedd reservoir (sailing and fishing) and rolling border country on doorstep.

Le4   Pontypridd

Busy Valleys town which recalls its past at the Pontypridd Historical and Cultural Centre. Mining traditions are also reflected at the nearby Rhondda Heritage Park. Pontypridd is Tom Jones's home town and singers Stewart Burrows and the late Sir Geraint Evans hail from nearby Cilfynydd. John Hughes's Grogg Shop with its sculptures of famous rugby players led to worldwide fame for his unique creations.

History comes to life at Llancaiach Fawr manor house, near Nelson

Blackwood   Caerphilly   Pontypool   Pontypridd

GH	Wyroed Lodge Guest House

Manmoel,
Blackwood
NP2 0RW
Tel: (01495) 371198

 COMMENDED

Old Victorian style farmhouse. Spacious en-suite rooms with tea and coffee making facilities, TV. Twin, double, family rooms, lounge, dining room for guests. Situated in small village with pub, church, playground, childrens park, beautiful views and walks. Ideal for touring, Cardiff. 45 minutes, Brecon 35 minutes and South Wales Valleys in general. Family run. Home cooking.

	SINGLE PER PERSON B&B	DOUBLE FOR 2 PERSONS B&B	🛏 3 🛁 3
	MIN £	MAX £	MIN £	MAX £	OPEN
	17.00	17.00	17.00	17.00	1-12

FH	Mill Farm

Cwmavon
NP4 8XJ
Tel: (01495) 774588

15th century farmhouse with oak beams, inglenooks, log fires, panelling. Furnished in keeping. All bedrooms en-suite with tea/coffee making facilities. Centrally heated, indoor heated pool with residents' lounge/TV room. The beautiful farmhouse is in an idyllic setting with gardens, grounds ideal for walking. Excellent base to explore South, Mid and West Wales.

	SINGLE PER PERSON B&B	DOUBLE FOR 2 PERSONS B&B	🛏 3 🛁 3
	MIN £	MAX £	MIN £	MAX £	OPEN
	-	20.00	-	40.00	1-12

FH	Wern Ganol Farm

Nelson,
Treharris
CF46 6PS
Tel: (01443) 450413

Sixty acre dairy farm on the main A4720. Pleasant views over surrounding countryside, towards Llancaiach Fawr Manor House. Easy access to Brecon Beacons. South Wales coast. Cardiff, Pontypridd, Caerphilly. Twenty minutes from M4, junction 32.

	SINGLE PER PERSON B&B	DOUBLE FOR 2 PERSONS B&B	🛏 5 🛁 5
	MIN £	MAX £	MIN £	MAX £	OPEN
	17.00	20.00	32.00	34.00	1-12

FH	Watford Fach Farm Guest House

Watford Road,
Caerphilly CF8 1NE
Tel: (01222) 851500
Fax: (01222) 865021

Close to Caerphilly Castle. En-suite rooms, central heating, ample parking, ground floor rooms. Rural setting, golf course nearby. Excellent breakfast. Friendly welcome. Welsh speaking owners.

	SINGLE PER PERSON B&B	DOUBLE FOR 2 PERSONS B&B	🛏 8 🛁 5
	MIN £	MAX £	MIN £	MAX £	OPEN
	15.00	18.00	30.00	30.00	1-12

Prices

In this publication we go to great lengths to make sure that you have a clear, accurate idea of prices and facilities. It's all spelled out in the 'Prices' section – and remember to confirm everything when making your booking.

Caerphilly Castle

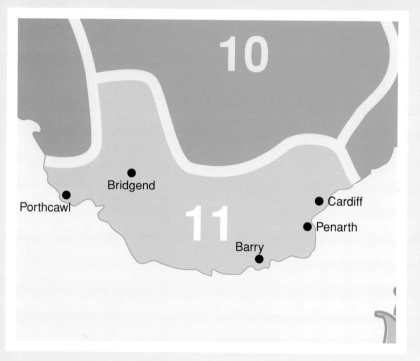

Cardiff is Wales's cosmopolitan capital city. It's a place of culture and the arts, with fine museums and theatres. It's also a city of great style – Cardiff's neoclassical civic architecture has won praise worldwide while the lavish city-centre castle, a seriously Victorian creation, never fails to astonish. The castle was built with the wealth generated by Cardiff's booming 19th-century seaport. The city is now renewing its maritime links through the exciting Cardiff Bay development, which is transforming the old waterfront. Close to the city there's attractive coast and countryside. The pastoral Vale of Glamorgan is dotted with picturesque villages and thatched cottages. And along the shore there's everything from the spectacular cliffs of the Glamorgan Heritage Coast to the popular resorts of Barry Island and Porthcawl.

It's a fact…

Cardiff was declared capital city of Wales in 1955. Its Victorian castle is built on the site of a 2000-year-old Roman fort. The Cardiff Bay development will create 8 miles of new waterfront and a 202-hectare/ 500-acre freshwater lake. Cardiff is only 2 hours by train from London. Cardiff-born author Roald Dahl was baptised in the city's Norwegian Church. The Glamorgan Heritage Coast, designated in 1973, runs for 14 miles between Aberthaw and Porthcawl. Merthyr Mawr has the highest sand dunes in Britain, rising to over 61m/200ft.

Ld5 Bridgend

Bustling commercial and market town on edge of rural Vale of Glamorgan. Lively resort of Porthcawl and unspoilt Heritage Coast with cliffs and dunes nearby. Beautiful Bryngarw Country Park and ancient Ewenny Priory on doorstep. Three ruined Norman castles in the area – Coity, Newcastle and Ogmore.

Le6 Cowbridge

Picturesque town with wide main street and pretty houses – the centre of the Vale of Glamorgan farming community. Fine old inns, shops selling high-class clothes and country wares. 14th-century town walls. Good touring centre for South Wales. Visit nearby Beaupre Castle.

Mb5 Cardiff

Capital of Wales, business, trade and entertainment centre. Splendid Civic Centre, lovely parkland, modern pedestrianised shopping centre, new waterfront development, good restaurants, theatres, cinemas, clubs and sports facilities, including ice-rink and Superbowl. Visit St David's Hall for top-class entertainment. Ornate city-centre castle. National Museum and Gallery has a fine collection of Impressionist paintings. Industrial and Maritime Museum and Techniquest science discovery centre on Cardiff Bay waterfront. National Stadium is home of Welsh rugby. Llandaff Cathedral close by and fascinating collection of old farmhouses and other buildings at the Museum of Welsh Life, St Fagans.

Lc6 Porthcawl

Traditional seaside resort – beaches, funfair, promenade. Attractive harbour and quieter coast along Rest Bay. Summer entertainment at the Grand Pavilion. Sailing and windsurfing. Famous golf course. Kenfig Pool and Dunes. Convenient for visiting unspoilt South Wales countryside – Bryngarw Country Park and Vale of Glamorgan with its attractive villages set amid leafy lanes.

Ld6 St Brides Major

Attractive village in the Vale of Glamorgan; spectacular Heritage Coast to the south. Close to Bridgend and ideal for visiting Ogmore Castle and Ewenny Priory. Golf at Southerndown.

Porthcawl

Bridgend Cardiff

GH The Garden House

Court Colman,
Pen-y-Fai,
Bridgend CF31 4NG
Tel: (01656) 725683

AWAITING INSPECTION

A comfortable friendly bed and breakfast offering family accommodation. Self-contained, own entrance. Children welcome. Situated in the countryside but close to M4 and main line railway station. Many good hotels, pubs and restaurants within short drive. Close to mountains and beaches. Golf, fishing and horseriding within a few miles. Colour TV.

		SINGLE PER PERSON B&B		DOUBLE FOR 2 PERSONS B&B		🛏 2 🛁 -
MIN £ 13.00	MAX £ 15.00	MIN £ 25.00	MAX £ 28.00	OPEN 1-12		

H Austins Hotel

11 Coldstream Terrace,
City Centre,
Cardiff CF1 8LJ
Tel: (01222) 377148

Small friendly hotel in the centre of the city. 200 yards from Cardiff Castle, first left over river bridge, overlooking the River Taff. Close to all amenities. Choice of rooms, including en-suite, available; colour TV and tea and coffee facilities in all bedrooms. Full English breakfast included. Warm welcome offered to all nationalities.

		SINGLE PER PERSON B&B		DOUBLE FOR 2 PERSONS B&B		🛏 11 🛁 3
MIN £ 14.00	MAX £ 20.00	MIN £ 26.00	MAX £ 32.00	OPEN 1-12		

H Courtfield Hotel

101 Cathedral Road,
Cardiff CF1 9PH
Tel: (01222) 227701
Fax: (01222) 227701

COMMENDED

Traditional Victorian town house hotel set in a fine conservation area, close to Cardiff Castle and city centre. AA Recommended. Accommodation from a choice of 15 well appointed bedrooms. All with central heating, private telephone, radio, colour TV, and hospitality tray. Full breakfast included. Popular lounge bar and restaurant. All major credit cards accepted.

		SINGLE PER PERSON B&B		DOUBLE FOR 2 PERSONS B&B		🛏 15 🛁 5
MIN £ 20.00	-	MIN £ 35.00	-	OPEN 1-12		

H Wynford Hotel

Clare Street,
Cardiff CF1 8SD
Tel: (01222) 371983
Fax: (01222) 340477

Very close to the city centre, train and bus stations, the Wynford, privately owned and personally supervised, offers a comfortable lounge, two cosy bars, occasional music and dancing, bistro and restaurant. All rooms have colour TV and telephone. Many have private bathroom. French Spanish and German spoken. Night porter. Video linked security car park. Price quoted relates to 7 rooms only.

		SINGLE PER PERSON B&B		DOUBLE FOR 2 PERSONS B&B		🛏 20 🛁 16
MIN £ 20.00	-	MIN £ 36.00	-	OPEN 1-12		

GH Bon Maison Guest House

39 Plasturton Gardens,
Cardiff
CF1 9HG
Tel: (01222) 383660

Situated in a lovely Victorian garden area, 1 mile from city centre, theatres and cinemas. Two rooms en-suite, two with shower. Comfortable lounge, no smoking area. Large varied breakfast menu catering for vegans also. All rooms have colour TV, heating, radio, and hospitality tray. Ironing facilities available. A very comfortable family run welcoming house.

		SINGLE PER PERSON B&B		DOUBLE FOR 2 PERSONS B&B		🛏 4 🛁 2
MIN £ 17.00	MAX £ 20.00	MIN £ 30.00	MAX £ 34.00	OPEN 1-12		

GH | Farthings

Lisvane Road, Lisvane,
Cardiff CF4 5SG
Tel: (01222) 756404
Fax: (01222) 387351

Close to Cardiff centre, yet in the heart of the village of Lisvane. "Farthings" offers double and single cottage style accommodation, private bathroom and lounge, plus secure parking. A few minutes' walk from the local inn, serving meals. Close to local rail and bus services direct to the city centre.

		SINGLE PER PERSON B&B		DOUBLE FOR 2 PERSONS B&B			2
		MIN £	MAX £	MIN £	MAX £	OPEN	-
		20.00	20.00	35.00	35.00	1-12	

FH | Cartreglas Farm

HIGHLY COMMENDED

Welsh St Donats,
Cowbridge CF7 7SX
Tel: (01446) 772368
Fax: (01446) 775553

A warm welcome awaits you at Cartreglas, where we grow flowers for drying. Conveniently situated for touring Cardiff, coast and mountains. In the lovely Vale of Glamorgan. 3 miles from junction 34 on M4 and 4 miles from Cowbridge. Fully equipped kitchen available for guests to make own evening meal. Children and pets welcome.

		SINGLE PER PERSON B&B		DOUBLE FOR 2 PERSONS B&B			3
		MIN £	MAX £	MIN £	MAX £	OPEN	3
		17.00	18.00	34.00	36.00	1-12	

GH | Westcliff House

3 West Drive,
Porthcawl
CF36 3LT
Tel: (01656) 782526

Premier position on the South Wales coast. Elegant house with spacious accommodation. All rooms have private facilities. Guaranteed parking. Ideally situated on west end of promenade. Non smoking. Ground floor room available. Colour TV's, tea making in all rooms. Ideal for all seasons. A warm welcome to all. Panoramic sea views.

		SINGLE PER PERSON B&B		DOUBLE FOR 2 PERSONS B&B			3
		MIN £	MAX £	MIN £	MAX £	OPEN	3
		-	-	36.00	40.00	1-12	

GH | Plas-y-Bryn

93 Fairwater Road,
Llandaff, Cardiff
CF5 2LS
Tel: (01222) 561717

HIGHLY COMMENDED

L

Comfortable Edwardian semi, outskirts Cardiff. Short walk from pretty village of Llandaff and cathedral, two minutes from Fairwater Station, Near buses. All home comforts, central heating, television, lounge, tea/coffee facilities. Also hand basins in bedrooms, which are quiet rooms. Good service. A48, M4 close by, also Folk Museum.

		SINGLE PER PERSON B&B		DOUBLE FOR 2 PERSONS B&B			3
		MIN £	MAX £	MIN £	MAX £	OPEN	-
		16.00	19.00	30.00	35.00	1-12	

H | Penoyre Private Hotel

29 Mary Street,
Porthcawl
CF36 3YN
Tel: (01656) 784550

Penoyre is a family run licensed hotel, 100 yards from beach and shopping centre. All rooms have colour TV, tea and coffee making facilities. En-suite available. Small friendly bar and TV lounge with satellite provided for guests' enjoyment. Children and pets welcome. Excellent home cooking, vegetarian and special diets on request. A la carte menu. RAC Acclaimed.

		SINGLE PER PERSON B&B		DOUBLE FOR 2 PERSONS B&B			7
		MIN £	MAX £	MIN £	MAX £	OPEN	4
		15.00	20.00	30.00	40.00	1-12	

FH | Penuchadre Farm

St Brides Major,
Bridgend
CF32 0TE
Tel: (01656) 880313

15th century historic farmhouse. High quality accommodation comprising one family bedroom. M4 motorway 5 miles (farmhouse easily found). Real farm atmosphere, wonderful for children. Heritage Coast, Southerndown Bay within walking distance. 18 hole championship golf course nearby. Evening meals available in local public houses. Idyllic countryside surroundings and a warm welcome awaits at Penuchadre Farm.

		SINGLE PER PERSON B&B		DOUBLE FOR 2 PERSONS B&B			1
		MIN £	MAX £	MIN £	MAX £	OPEN	-
		18.00	18.00	36.00	36.00	1-12	

GH | Villa Guest House

27 Mary Street,
Porthcawl
CF36 3YN
Tel: (01656) 785074

Small, friendly, family run guest house, centrally situated to all of Porthcawl's attractions. All bedrooms have remote controlled colour TV's, tea/coffee facilities, shower. En-suite available in several rooms. Warm and comfortable. An ideal base for touring the South Wales countryside.

		SINGLE PER PERSON B&B		DOUBLE FOR 2 PERSONS B&B			6
		MIN £	MAX £	MIN £	MAX £	OPEN	3
		13.00	14.00	24.00	34.00	1-12	

Pets welcome

You'll see from the symbols that many places to stay welcome dogs and pets by prior arrangement. Although some sections of beach may have restrictions, there are always adjacent areas – the promenade, for example, or quieter stretches of sands – where dogs can be exercised on and sometimes off leads. Please ask at a Tourist Information Centre for advice.

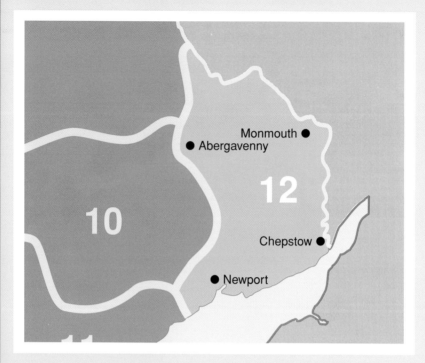

These two lovely valleys, close to the border, serve as the best possible introduction to Wales. The thickly wooded Wye Valley snakes its way northwards from Chepstow through countryside which is beautiful in all seasons. It's a walker's paradise, with a wonderful choice of trails including woodland, riverside and Offa's Dyke paths. Rolling green hills separate the Wye from the Usk, another beautiful river valley which reaches the sea at Newport.

Fishermen, as well as walkers, love this part of Wales, for both rivers are famed for their salmon and trout. These borderlands, a natural gateway into Wales over the centuries, are dotted with historic sites of great significance – the Roman town of Caerleon, castles at almost every turn, and the splendid 17th-century mansion of Tredegar House, Newport.

It's a fact...

The Wye Valley between Chepstow and Monmouth is an 'Area of Outstanding Natural Beauty', designated in 1971. Britain's first stone-built castle was constructed at Chepstow in 1067. Charles Stewart Rolls, of Rolls-Royce celebrity, is a famous son of Monmouth – his statue stands in the town square. The majestic ruin of Tintern Abbey was founded in 1131 by Cistercian monks. The floral town of Usk is a regular 'Wales in Bloom ' winner. Monmouth's fortified Monnow Bridge is the only one of its kind in Britain.

Mc1 Abergavenny

Flourishing market town with backdrop of mountains at south-eastern gateway to Brecon Beacons National Park. Pony trekking in nearby Black Mountains. Castle, Museum of Childhood and Home. Leisure centre. Monmouthshire and Brecon Canal runs just to the west of the town. Excellent touring base for the lovely Vale of Usk and Brecon Beacons.

Me4 Chepstow

Attractive hilly town with substantial remains of a great stone castle – reputedly the first to be built in Britain – above the Wye. Fortified gate still stands in main street and medieval walls remain. Good shopping. Museum, Stuart Crystal Engraving Workshop. Sunday market, fine racecourse, excellent walks – beginning of the Wye Valley Walk and Offa's Dyke Path. Ideal for touring beautiful Wye Valley.

Mc3 Cwmbran

A 'new town' development and administrative centre. Good leisure facilities. Llantarnam Grange Arts Centre. Shopping and sports centre with international athletics stadium. Theatre and cinemas. Well-located touring centre for the Vale of Usk and South Wales Valleys.

Me1 Monmouth

Historic market town in picturesque Wye Valley – birthplace of Henry V and Charles Rolls (of Rolls-Royce). Interesting local history museum with collection of Nelson memorabilia. Rare fortified gateway still spans the River Monnow. Ruined castle close to town centre. Well located for touring Wye Valley and borderland Wales.

Mc4 Newport

Busy industrial, commercial and shopping centre. Interesting murals in main hall of Civic Centre. Newport Museum and Art Gallery in John Frost Square (named after Chartist leader) and leisure centre with wave machine. On the outskirts, magnificently restored Tredegar House with extensive country park, and 14 Locks Canal Visitor Centre. St Woolos Cathedral on hill overlooking town centre. Ruined castle on riverside near shops and attractive Victorian market hall.

Md2 Raglan

Historic village dominated by Raglan Castle, noted for its impressive Great Tower of Gwent. Convenient for touring the Usk and Wye valleys and eastern Brecon Beacons.

Mc5 St Brides Wentloog

Settlement on mouth of Usk close to Newport overlooking Severn Estuary. Splendid Tredegar House and Country Park nearby; Cardiff only a short distance away.

Me3 Tintern

Riverside village in particularly lovely stretch of Wye Valley. Impressive ruins of Tintern Abbey not to be missed. The former railway station has a visitors' interpretive centre and picnic site with refreshments. Excellent walks and good fishing.

Md3 Usk

Ancient borough on River Usk; excellent salmon fishing and inns. Good walks. Rural Life Museum, grass skiing. Great castle of Raglan 5 miles north. Sailing and other watersports on nearby Llandegfedd reservoir. Good central location for sightseeing.

Abergavenny   Chepstow   Cwmbran   Monmouth

H	Rock & Fountain Hotel

Clydach,   **COMMENDED**
Abergavenny
NP7 0LL
Tel: (01873) 830393

Brecon Beacons National Park, 16th century family run hotel, situated in the famous Clydach Gorge. The hotel has breathtaking views with riding, golf, fishing and canal boating nearby. The beautiful featured restaurant offers home cooked meals using fresh local produce. Lovely walks in a tranquil setting pass the front door. These you must try.

P C	SINGLE PER PERSON B&B	DOUBLE FOR 2 PERSONS B&B	🛏 9
			9
	MIN £ 20.00	MAX £ 20.00	MIN £ 35.00	MAX £ 40.00	OPEN 1-12

FH	High House Farm

Bryngwyn,   **HIGHLY COMMENDED**
Raglan
NP5 2BS
Tel: (01291) 690529

A traditional Welsh farmhouse nestling close to the Usk and Wye Valleys and within easy reach of the Brecon Beacons National Park. Three extremely comfortable bedrooms compliment the beamed dining room and guests' sitting room, enjoying extensive views of the Black Mountains. High House is a working dairy farm, with ample parking facilities.

P	SINGLE PER PERSON B&B	DOUBLE FOR 2 PERSONS B&B	🛏 3
			1
	MIN £ 16.00	MAX £ 18.00	MIN £ 32.00	MAX £ 36.00	OPEN 3-10

GH	The Old Rectory

Tintern,
Chepstow
NP6 6SG
Tel: (01291) 689519

A free and easy welcome awaits you at this imposing 18/19th century house with its own spring water. Most bedrooms have beautiful views, H&C, tea/coffee facilities. Central heating, log fires and dining room serving good food, own bread and produce in season. Central for fishing, walking, golf, horse riding. Tintern Abbey 0.5 miles. Ideal for touring the border country.

P	SINGLE PER PERSON B&B	DOUBLE FOR 2 PERSONS B&B	🛏 4
			-
	MIN £ 14.50	MAX £ 14.50	MIN £ 29.00	MAX £ 29.00	OPEN 1-12

GH	Heathfield

Nant-y-Derry,   **HIGHLY COMMENDED**
Abergavenny
NP7 9DP
Tel: (01873) 880675

Country house set in a large garden with a croquet lawn. Views of the Blorenge Mountain. Comfortable and spacious rooms, all centrally heated with tea/coffee facilities. Evening meals on request. TV lounge to relax in. 5 miles from Abergavenny, 4 miles from Usk. Scenic walks in peaceful countryside, excellent golf course, two minutes away

P	SINGLE PER PERSON B&B	DOUBLE FOR 2 PERSONS B&B	🛏 3
			1
	MIN £ -	MAX £ -	MIN £ 30.00	MAX £ 36.00	OPEN 3-11

FH	Wern Gochlyn Farm

Llantilio Pertholey,   **APPROVED**
Abergavenny
NP7 8BW
Tel: (01873) 857357

12th century farmhouse 2 miles from market town of Abergavenny, under Skirrid Mountain. En-suite bedrooms, 1 double, 1 family. Tea/coffee making facilities. Approved riding centre with instructor, indoor heated swimming pool, games room. Good walks through farm, 0.5 miles 18 hole golf course and golf range. Friendly farm animals. Famous Walnut Tree Restaurant 0.5 miles. Brochure.

P	SINGLE PER PERSON B&B	DOUBLE FOR 2 PERSONS B&B	🛏 2
			2
	MIN £ 20.00	MAX £ -	MIN £ 32.00	MAX £ 36.00	OPEN 1-12

GH	Springfields

371 Llantarnam Road,   **HIGHLY COMMENDED**
Llantarnam,
Cwmbran
NP44 3BN
Tel: (01633) 482509

Family rum for 23 happy years. 1.5 miles from Cwmbran, 2.5 miles M4, junction 25A. Central for touring Wye Valley, Big Pit, Caerleon, Cardiff. My visitors have enjoyed Springfields, I have enjoyed their company. Come and see the beauty of South Wales. You will come again. Thank you old and new customers, Joan Graham. Six rooms en-suite.

P	SINGLE PER PERSON B&B	DOUBLE FOR 2 PERSONS B&B	🛏 10
			6
	MIN £ -	MAX £ 16.50	MIN £ -	MAX £ 32.00	OPEN 1-12

GH	Pentre House

Brecon Road,   **HIGHLY COMMENDED**
Abergavenny
NP7 7EW
Tel: (01873) 853435
Fax: (01873) 853435

Small period country house situated at the turning for Sugar Loaf, just off A40. Set in 1 acre of award winning gardens. Guest bathroom and shower room. Sitting room with wood burning stove. Very comfortably furnished peaceful surroundings. River Usk just down the lane. Pony trekking, golf, lovely walks, all nearby. Brochure available.

P C	SINGLE PER PERSON B&B	DOUBLE FOR 2 PERSONS B&B	🛏 3
			-
	MIN £ 15.00	MAX £ 20.00	MIN £ 28.00	MAX £ 36.00	OPEN 1-12

GH	Llanishen House

Llanishen,
Chepstow
NP6 6QS
Tel: (01600) 860700

Relax in an Area of Outstanding Natural Beauty, with many local forest walks and panoramic views. Convenient to the historic towns of Chepstow, Monmouth, Usk and Tintern. Recently refurbished converted stables overlooking picturesque courtyard, adjacent to 17th century country house, set in secluded grounds. Private suite consists of sitting room, twin bedded room and bathroom.

P	SINGLE PER PERSON B&B	DOUBLE FOR 2 PERSONS B&B	🛏 1
			1
	MIN £ -	MAX £ -	MIN £ 38.00	MAX £ -	OPEN 1-12

GH	Church Farm Guest House

Mitchel Troy,   **COMMENDED**
Monmouth
NP5 4HZ
Tel: (01600) 712176

A spacious and homely 16th century former farmhouse with oak beams and inglenook fireplaces. Set in large attractive garden with stream. Easy access to A40 and only 2 miles from historic Monmouth. Excellent base for Wye Valley, Forest of Dean and Black Mountains. Large car park. terrace, barbeque, colour TV, central heating, tea/coffee making facilities.

P	SINGLE PER PERSON B&B	DOUBLE FOR 2 PERSONS B&B	🛏 8
			6
	MIN £ 17.00	MAX £ 19.50	MIN £ 34.00	MAX £ 39.00	OPEN 1-12

FH | Mill House Farm

Llanvihangel-Ystern-Llewern,
Monmouth
NP5 4HN
Tel: (01600) 780468

16th century farmhouse set in lovely gardens, located between Monmouth and Abergavenny. The Wye and Usk Valleys, Offa's Dyke, Forest of Dean, and the Black Mountains are all close by. Activities include golf, fishing, walking, canoeing and pony trekking. Tea and coffee in all rooms. Evening meals available, vegetarians welcome.

		SINGLE PER PERSON B&B	DOUBLE FOR 2 PERSONS B&B		3
					1
MIN £	MAX £	MIN £	MAX £	OPEN	
16.00	16.00	32.00	36.00	1-12	

FH | Brooklands Farm

Chepstow Road,
Raglan
NP5 2EN
Tel: (01291) 690782

Family run dairy farm with sheep and cattle. Situated close to Raglan Castle and within 200 metres of Raglan village, with its shops and pubs. Rooms available: one double en-suite/family room, two twin rooms, one single room. TV lounge overlooking large garden for relaxing in the sunshine.

		SINGLE PER PERSON B&B	DOUBLE FOR 2 PERSONS B&B		4
					1
MIN £	MAX £	MIN £	MAX £	OPEN	
14.00	18.00	28.00	36.00	1-12	

GH | Valley House

COMMENDED

Raglan Road,
Tintern NP6 6TH
Tel: (01291) 689652
Fax: (01291) 689805

18th century detached house in picturesque valley just 800m off A466, within one mile of Tintern Abbey. Beautiful en-suite rooms with colour TV's, radios, tea/coffee facilities and telephones. Freshly cooked hearty breakfasts, packed lunches available. Ideal base for touring Wye Valley. Forest walks from our doorstep. Numerous places to eat nearby.

		SINGLE PER PERSON B&B	DOUBLE FOR 2 PERSONS B&B		3
					3
MIN £	MAX £	MIN £	MAX £	OPEN	
26.00	26.00	36.00	36.00	1-12	

FH | Pentre-Tai Farm

HIGHLY COMMENDED

Rhiwderin,
Newport
NP1 9RQ
Tel: (01633) 893284

Situated 3 miles from junction 28, M4 and 12 miles from Cardiff. Welcome to our peaceful sheep and horse farm. En-suite rooms. Special rates for children. One family room. All rooms with colour TV and tea/coffee facilities. Excellent pub food nearby. Ideal for visiting Wye Valley, Brecon Beacons, wonderful Welsh castles and South Wales coast.

		SINGLE PER PERSON B&B	DOUBLE FOR 2 PERSONS B&B		3
					2
MIN £	MAX £	MIN £	MAX £	OPEN	
20.00	20.00	32.00	34.00	2-11	

GH | Chapel Guest House

 COMMENDED

Church Road,
St Brides Wentloog
NP1 9SN
Tel: (01633) 681018

Comfortable en-suite accommodation in a converted chapel situated in village between Newport/Cardiff. Inn/restaurant adjacent. Pleasant walks, fishing, golf, horse riding, nearby. Guest lounge with pool table. Beverage trays, TV, in all rooms. Children welcome, special rates. Leave M4 junction 28, take A48 Newport, at roundabout take 3rd exit B4239 St Brides. Centre of village opposite Church House Inn.

		SINGLE PER PERSON B&B	DOUBLE FOR 2 PERSONS B&B		3
					3
MIN £	MAX £	MIN £	MAX £	OPEN	
17.00	19.00	30.00	34.00	1-12	

FH | Ty-Gwyn Farm

 AWARD **HIGHLY COMMENDED**

Gwehelog,
Usk
NP5 1RT
Tel: (01291) 672878

Wake up and sit up to magnificent views of Brecon Beacons National Park at this award winning farmhouse. Hearty breakfasts including homemade preserves served in spacious dining room or conservatory overlooking secluded lawns. Tea making facilities and TV in bedrooms. Explore castles, mountains, rivers, golf courses and fishing nearby. Excellent meals, vegetarians and own wine welcome. Brochure available.

		SINGLE PER PERSON B&B	DOUBLE FOR 2 PERSONS B&B		3
					2
MIN £	MAX £	MIN £	MAX £	OPEN	
-	-	30.00	38.00	1-12	

Award-winning farmhouses and guest houses

Look out for the Wales Tourist Board Award on the pages of this guide. Award winners offer extra-special standards of comfort, furnishings and surroundings. They're as good as many a hotel. And proprietors will have completed college training in tourism.

Monmouth

Make the most of your stay in Wales by contacting one of our Tourist Information Centres for help on all aspects of your holiday. TIC staff will be delighted to assist with:
● booking your accommodation (*see below*) ● places to visit ● places to eat ● things to do
● routes to take ● national and local events ● maps, guides and books

Tourist Information Centres

Normal opening times are 10am–30pm. These hours may vary to suit local circumstances. Those marked with an asterisk (*) are open seasonally only (April–September).

The Bed Booking Service is free for local reservations. A £1 fee applies to bookings made further afield in Wales.

Aberaeron	The Quay, Aberaeron SA46 0BT	Tel (01545) 570602
Aberdovey/Aberdyfi *	Wharf Gardens, Aberdovey LL35 0ED	Tel (01654) 767321
Abergavenny *	Swan Meadow, Monmouth Road, Abergavenny NP7 5HH	Tel (01873) 857588
Aberystwyth	Terrace Road, Aberystwyth SY23 2AG	Tel (01970) 612125
Bala	Penllyn, Pensarn Road, Bala LL23 7SR	Tel (01678) 521021
Bangor *	Little Chef Services, A55/A5 Llandygai, Bangor LL57 7BG	Tel (01248) 352786
Barmouth *	Old Library, Station Road, Barmouth LL42 1LU	Tel (01341) 280787
Barry Island *	The Triangle, Paget Road, Barry Island CF62 8TJ	Tel (01446) 747171
Betws-y-Coed	Royal Oak Stables, Betws-y-Coed LL24 0AH	Tel (01690) 710426
Blaenau Ffestiniog *	Isallt, High Street, Blaenau Ffestiniog LL41 3HD	Tel (01766) 830360
Borth *	High Street, The Promenade, Borth SY24 5HY	Tel (01970) 871174
Brecon	Cattle Market Car Park, Brecon LD3 9DA	Tel (01874) 622485
Builth Wells	Groe Car Park, Builth Wells LD2 3BT	Tel (01982) 553307
Caerleon	High Street, Caerleon	Tel (01633) 422656
Caernarfon	Oriel Pendeitsh, Castle Street, Caernarfon LL55 2NA	Tel (01286) 672232
Caerphilly	Twyn Square, Caerphilly	Tel (01222) 851378
Cardiff	Central Station, Cardiff CF1 1QY	Tel (01222) 227281
Cardigan	Theatr Mwldan, Bath House Road, Cardigan SA43 2JY	Tel (01239) 613230
Carmarthen	Lammas Street, Carmarthen SA31 3AQ	Tel (01267) 231557
Chepstow	Castle Car Park, Bridge Street, Chepstow NP6 5EY	Tel (01291) 623772
Colwyn Bay	40 Station Road, Colwyn Bay LL29 8BU	Tel (01492) 530478
Conwy	Conwy Castle Visitor Centre, Conwy LL32 8LD	Tel (01492) 592248
Corris *	Craft Centre, Corris, nr Machynlleth SY20 9SP	Tel (01654) 761244
Crickhowell *	Beaufort Chambers, Beaufort Street, Crickhowell NP8 1AA	Tel (01873) 812105
Cwmcarn	Visitor Centre, Cwmcarn Forest Drive, nr Cross Keys NP1 7FA	Tel (01495) 272001
Dolgellau	Tŷ Meirion, Eldon Square, Dolgellau LL40 1PU	Tel (01341) 422888
Elan Valley *	Elan Valley Visitor Centre, Elan Valley, nr Rhayader LD6 5HP	Tel (01597) 810898
Ewloe	Autolodge Services, A55 Westbound, Northophall, Ewloe CH7 6HE	Tel (01244) 541597
Fishguard Harbour	Passenger Concourse, The Harbour, Goodwick, Fishguard SA64 0BU	Tel (01348) 872037
Fishguard Town	4 Hamilton Street, Fishguard SA65 9HL	Tel (01348) 873484
Harlech *	Gwyddfor House, High Street, Harlech LL46 2YA	Tel (01766) 780658
Haverfordwest	Old Bridge, Haverfordwest SA61 2EZ	Tel (01437) 763110
Holyhead	Marine Square, Salt Island Approach, Holyhead LL65 1DR	Tel (01407) 762622
Kilgetty *	Kingsmoor Common, Kilgetty SA68 0YA	Tel (01834) 813672
Knighton	Offa's Dyke Centre, West Street, Knighton LD7 1EW	Tel (01547) 528753
Lake Vyrnwy	Unit 2, Vyrnwy Craft Workshops, Lake Vyrnwy SY10 0LY	Tel (01691) 870346
Llanberis *	41 High Street, Llanberis	Tel (01286) 870765
Llandarcy *	BP Club, Llandarcy, Neath SA10 6HJ	Tel (01792) 813030
Llandovery *	Central Car Park, Broad Street, Llandovery SA20 0AR	Tel (01550) 720693

Llandrindod Wells	Old Town Hall, Memorial Gardens, Llandrindod Wells LD1 5DL	Tel (01597) 822600
Llandudno	1-2 Chapel Street, Llandudno LL30 2YU	Tel (01492) 876413
Llanelli	Public Library, Vaughan Street, Llanelli SA15 3AS	Tel (01554) 772020
Llanfairpwllgwyngyll	Station Site, Llanfairpwllgwyngyll LL61 5UJ	Tel (01248) 713177
Llangollen	Town Hall, Castle Street, Llangollen LL20 5PD	Tel (01978) 860828
Llanidloes	Town Hall, Great Oak Street, Llanidloes SY18 6BN	Tel (01686) 412605
Llanwrtyd Wells	Tŷ Barcud, The Square, Llanwrtyd Wells LD5 4RB	Tel (01591) 610666
Machynlleth	Canolfan Owain Glyndŵr, Machynlleth SY20 8EE	Tel (01654) 702401
Magor	Granada Services West, Junction 23 M4, Magor NP6 3YL	Tel (01633) 881122
Merthyr Tydfil	14a Glebeland Street, Merthyr Tydfil CF47 8AU	Tel (01685) 379884
Milford Haven *	94 Charles Street, Milford Haven SA73 2HL	Tel (01646) 690866
Mold	Library, Museum and Art Gallery, Earl Road, Mold CH7 1AP	Tel (01352) 759331
Monmouth *	Shire Hall, Agincourt Square, Monmouth NP5 3DY	Tel (01600) 713899
Mumbles *	Oystermouth Square, Mumbles, Swansea SA3 4DQ	Tel (01792) 361302
Narberth	Town Hall, Narberth SA67 7AR	Tel (01834) 860061
New Quay *	Church Street, New Quay SA45 9NZ	Tel (01545) 560865
Newcastle Emlyn *	Market Hall, Newcastle Emlyn SA38 9AE	Tel (01239) 711333
Newport	Newport Museum & Art Gallery, John Frost Square, Newport NP9 1HZ	Tel (01633) 842962
Newtown	Central Car Park, Newtown SY16 2PW	Tel (01686) 625580
Pembroke	Visitor Centre, Commons Road, Pembroke SA71 4EA	Tel (01646) 622388
Pembroke Dock *	Guntower, Front Street	Tel (01646) 622246
Penarth *	Penarth Pier, The Esplanade, Penarth CF64 3AU	Tel (01222) 708849
Pont Abraham	Pont Abraham Services, Junction 49 M4, Llanedi SA4 1FP	Tel (01792) 883838
Pontardawe	3 Herbert Street, Pontardawe	Tel (01792) 864475
Pont Nedd Fechan	nr Glyn Neath SA11 5NR	Tel (01639) 721795
Pontypridd	Historical and Cultural Centre, The Old Bridge, Pontypridd CF37 3PE	Tel (01443) 409512
Porthcawl	Old Police Station, John Street, Porthcawl CF36 3DT	Tel (01656) 786639
Porthmadog	High Street, Porthmadog LL49 9LP	Tel (01766) 512981
Prestatyn *	Scala Cinema, High Street, Prestatyn LL19 9LH	Tel (01745) 889092
Presteigne *	Old Market Hall, Broad Street, Presteigne LD8 2AW	Tel (01544) 260193
Pwllheli	Min y Don, Station Square, Pwllheli LL53 5HG	Tel (01758) 613000
Rhayader	Leisure Centre, Rhayader LD6 5BU	Tel (01597) 810591
Rhos on Sea *	The Promenade, Rhos on Sea LL28 4EP	Tel (01492) 548778
Rhyl	Rhyl Children's Village, West Parade, Rhyl LL18 1HZ	Tel (01745) 355068
Ruthin	Ruthin Craft Centre, Park Road, Ruthin LL15 1BB	Tel (01824) 703992
St David's *	City Hall, St David's SA62 6SD	Tel (01437) 720392
Sarn	Sarn Park Services, Junction 36 M4, nr Bridgend CF32 9SY	Tel (01656) 654906
Swansea	PO Box 59, Singleton Street, Swansea SA1 3QG	Tel (01792) 468321
Tenby	The Croft, Tenby SA70 8AP	Tel (01834) 842402
Tregaron	The Square, Tregaron SY25 6JN	Tel (01974) 298144
Tywyn *	High Street, Tywyn LL36 9AD	Tel (01654) 710070
Welshpool	Flash Leisure Centre, Salop Road, Welshpool SY21 7DH	Tel (01938) 552043
Wrexham	Lambpit Street, Wrexham LL11 1AY	Tel (01978) 292015

And at Oswestry on the Wales/England border

Heritage Centre	2 Church Terrace, Oswestry SY11 2TE	Tel (01691) 662753
Mile End Services	Oswestry SY11 4JA	Tel (01691) 662488

Wales in London's West End

If you're in London, call in at the Wales Information Bureau, British Travel Centre, 12 Lower Regent Street, Piccadilly Circus, London SW1Y 4PQ. Tel (0171) 409 0969. Staff there will give you all the information you need to plan your visit to Wales.

Further Information

Travel facts

By rail

Please contact your local travel agent or principal stations:

Birmingham – Tel (0121) 643 2711

Cardiff – Tel (01222) 228000

London (to North Wales) – Tel (0171) 387 7070

London (to South Wales) – Tel (0171) 262 6767

Manchester – Tel (0161) 832 8353

There are eight members of Wales's narrow-gauge 'Great Little Trains': Bala Lake Railway, Brecon Mountain Railway (Merthyr Tydfil), Ffestiniog Railway (Porthmadog), Llanberis Lake Railway, Talyllyn Railway (Tywyn), Vale of Rheidol Railway (Aberystwyth), Welsh Highland Railway (Porthmadog) and Welshpool and Llanfair Railway (Llanfair Caereinion). 'Great Little Trains' details are available from The Station, Llanfair Caereinion SY21 0SF (tel 01938-810441).

The railways operating independently of 'Great Little Trains' are: Fairbourne and Barmouth Steam Railway (tel 01341-250362), Gwili Railway, nr Carmarthen (tel 01267-230666), Llangollen Railway (tel 01978-860951), Snowdon Mountain Railway, Llanberis (tel 01286-870223) and Teifi Valley Railway, nr Newcastle Emlyn (tel 01559-371077).

By coach

Contact your local travel agent or National Express office. For all National Express enquiries please telephone the Nationalcall number (0990) 808080 (calls cost a maximum of 10p per minute, less at off-peak times).

By sea

Five services operate across the Irish Sea:

Cork to Swansea (Swansea-Cork Ferries, tel 01792-456116)

Dublin to Holyhead (Irish Ferries, tel 0151-227 3131)

Dun Laoghaire to Holyhead (Stena Sealink – a choice of three services: High-Speed Superferry, tel 01233-615455, Sea Lynx Catamaran, tel 01233-647047, and Ferry, tel 01233-647047)

Rosslare to Fishguard (Stena Sealink – a choice of two services: Sea Lynx Catamaran and Ferry, tel 01233-647047)

Rosslare to Pembroke Dock (Irish Ferries, tel 0151-227 3132)

By air

There are direct flights from Aberdeen, Amsterdam, Belfast, Brussels, Channel Islands, Dublin, Edinburgh, Glasgow, Isle of Man, Manchester and Paris to Cardiff International Airport (tel 01446-711111), 12 miles from the city centre. Connecting services worldwide are via Amsterdam. Manchester and Birmingham Airports are also convenient gateways for Wales.

Gwyliau Cymru/ Festivals of Wales

This is the collective voice for over 50 arts festivals, embracing everything from classical music to jazz, children's events to drama. *For more information, please contact:* Festivals of Wales, Red House, Newtown SY16 3LE Tel (01686) 626442

The following organisations and authorities will be pleased to provide any further information you require when planning your holiday to Wales.

Wales Tourist Board, Dept BBG, Davis Street, Cardiff CF1 2FU Tel (01222) 475226

(Holiday and travel information is available from the above address, together with a free leaflet explaining the WTB's 'Quest for Quality' inspection schemes.)

Holiday information is also available from:

North Wales Tourism, Dept BBG, 77 Conway Road, Colwyn Bay LL29 7BL Tel (01492) 531731 Holiday Bookings (0800) 834820

Mid Wales Tourism, Dept BBG, The Station, Machynlleth SY20 8TG Tel (01654) 702653 Holiday Bookings (0800) 273747

Tourism South and West Wales, Dept BBG, Charter Court, Enterprise Park, Swansea SA7 9DB Tel (01792) 781212 (quote Dept BBG) Holiday Bookings (0800) 243731

Tourism South and West Wales, Dept BBG, Old Bridge, Haverfordwest, Pembrokeshire SA62 2EZ Tel (01437) 766330 (quote Dept BBG) Holiday Bookings (0800) 243731

Wales on the Internet

A wide range of travel and holiday information on Wales is now available on the Wales Tourist Board's Internet address:

www.tourism.wales.gov.uk

Other useful addresses

Brecon Beacons National Park,
Park Office, 7 Glamorgan Street,
Brecon LD3 7DP
Tel (01874) 624437

Cadw: Welsh Historic Monuments,
Brunel House, 2 Fitzalan Road,
Cardiff CF2 1UY
Tel (01222) 465511

Football Association of Wales,
3 Westgate Street, Cardiff CF1 1DD
Tel (01222) 372325

Forestry Enterprise (Forestry Commission),
Victoria House, Victoria Terrace,
Aberystwyth SY23 2DQ
Tel (01970) 612367

National Trust,
North Wales Regional Office,
Trinity Square,
Llandudno LL30 2DE
Tel (01492) 860123

National Trust,
South Wales Regional Office,
The King's Head, Bridge Street,
Llandeilo SA19 6BB
Tel (01558) 822800

National Rivers Authority,
(Fisheries and Conservation
enquiries), Plas-yr-Afon,
St Mellons Business Park,
St Mellons, Cardiff CF3 0LT
Tel (01222) 770088

Offa's Dyke Centre,
West Street, Knighton LD7 1EN
Tel (01547) 528753

Pembrokeshire Coast National Park,
National Park Department,
County Offices, St Thomas Green,
Haverfordwest SA61 1QZ
Tel (01437) 764591

Ramblers' Association in Wales,
Ty'r Cerddwyr, High Street,
Gresford, Wrexham LL12 8PT
Tel (01978) 855148

Snowdonia National Park,
Snowdonia National Park Office,
Penrhyndeudraeth LL48 6LS
Tel (01766) 770274

Surfcall Wales
(daily surf/weather conditions at
all major beaches)
Tel (0839) 505697/360361
Calls cost 39p per minute cheap
rate, 49p per minute at all other
times

Taste of Wales-*Blas ar Gymru*,
Welsh Food Promotions Ltd,
Cardiff Business Technology
Centre, Senghenydd Road,
Cardiff CF2 4AY
Tel (01222) 640456

Wales Craft Council,
Park Lane House, 7 High Street,
Welshpool SY21 7JP
Tel (01938) 555313

Welsh Golfing Union,
Catsafh, Newport NP6 1JQ
Tel (01633) 430830

Welsh Rugby Union,
Cardiff Arms Park, PO Box 22,
Cardiff CF1 1JL
Tel (01222) 390111

Youth Hostels Association,
1 Cathedral Road,
Cardiff CF1 9HA
Tel (01222) 396766

We'll show you around

The Wales Official Tourist Guides
offer an expert guiding service at
very reasonable fees – from
hourly tours by car or coach to
extended tours of any duration
throughout Wales. WOTG guides
and driver/guides are the only
qualified tourist guides in Wales,
and the association is registered
with the Wales Tourist Board.
Further details from:
Derek Jones,
Y Stabl, 30 Acton Gardens,
Box Lane, Wrexham LL12 8DE
Tel (01978) 351212
Fax (01978) 363060

Information for visitors with disabilities

The wheelchair accessibility
guidelines in the 'Where to Stay'
sections of this publication are
designed to provide reliable and
consistent information through
standardised inspection schemes.
All properties in this book
identified as being accessible to
disabled visitors have been
inspected by the Wales Tourist
Board.

Discovering Accessible Wales is an
information-packed guide for
visitors who may have impaired
movement or are confined to a
wheelchair. The book is available
free from the Wales Tourist Board.
See 'Guides and Maps' at the end
of this publication for details.

For details of other wheelchair-
accessible accommodation
inspected to the same standards
please contact the Holiday Care
Service. This organisation also
provides a wide range of other
travel and holiday information
for disabled visitors:

Holiday Care Service,
2nd Floor, Imperial Buildings,
Victoria Road, Horley,
Surrey RH6 7PZ
Tel (01293) 774535

Other helpful organisations

Wales Council for the Blind,
Shand House, 20 Newport Road,
Cardiff CF2 1DB
Tel (01222) 473954

Wales Council for the Deaf,
Maritime Offices,
Woodland Terrace, Maes-y-Coed,
Pontypridd CF37 1DZ
Tel (01443) 485687
Minicom (01443) 485686

Disability Wales,
Llys Ifor, Crescent Road,
Caerphilly CF83 1XL
Tel (01222) 887325/6/7/8

Trespass – a word of warning
If you're out and about enjoying
an activity holiday – walking off
established footpaths, mountain
biking, or even landing your
paraglider! – please obtain
permission from landowners. To
avoid any problems, it's always
best to seek out the appropriate
permission beforehand.

British Tourist Authority Overseas Offices

Your enquiries will be welcome at the offices of the British Tourist Authority in the following countries:

ARGENTINA
British Tourist Authority, 2nd Floor,
Avenida Cordoba 645,
1054 Buenos Aires
(open to the public 1000-1400 only)
Tel (1) 314 5514   Fax(1) 314 8955

AUSTRALIA
British Tourist Authority, 8th Floor,
University Centre, 210 Clarence Street,
Sydney, NSW 2000
Tel (2) 261 607   Fax (2) 267 4442

BELGIUM
British Tourist Authority,
306 Avenue Louise,
1050 Brussels
Tel (2) 646 35 10   Fax (2) 646 39 86

CANADA
British Tourist Authority,
111 Avenue Road,
Suite 450, Toronto, Ontario M5R 3J8
Tel (416) 925 6326   Fax (416) 961 2175

CZECH AND SLOVAK REPUBLICS
British Tourist Authority, Kaprova 13,
110 01 Prague 1, PO Box 264
Tel (2) 232 7213   Fax (2) 232 7469

DENMARK
British Tourist Authority, Montergade 3,
1116 Copenhagen K
Tel 33 91 88

FRANCE
Tourisme de Grande-Bretagne,
Maison de la Grande-Bretagne,
19 rue des Mathurins, 75009 Paris
(entre les rues Tronchet et Auber)
Tel 44 51 56 20   Fax 44 51 56 21
Minjtel 3615 BRITISH

GERMANY
British Tourist Authority,
Taunusstrasse 52-60,
60329 Frankfurt
Tel (69) 2380711   Fax (69) 2380717

GREECE
Action Public Relations, Kritonos 23,
Pangratu, GR 161-21
Tel (1) 72 40 160   Fax (1) 72 23 417

HONG KONG
British Tourist Authority, Room 1504,
Eton Tower, 8 Hysan Avenue,
Causeway Bay, Hong Kong
Tel 2882 9967   Fax 2577 1443

IRELAND
British Tourist Authority,
18-19 College Green, Dublin 2
Tel (1) 670 8000   Fax (1) 670 8244

ITALY
British Tourist Authority,
Corso V. Emanuele 337,
00186 Rome
Tel (6) 68806464   Fax (6) 6879095
(solo ricezione)

JAPAN
British Tourist Authority,
Tokyo Club Building,
3-2-6 Kasumigaseki, Chiyoda-ku,
Tokyo 100
Tel (3) 3581 3603/4   Fax (3) 3581 5797

NETHERLANDS
British Tourist Authority,
Aurora Gebouw (5e),
Stadhouderskade 2, 1054 ES Amsterdam
Tel (2) 685 50 51

NEW ZEALAND
British Tourist Authority, Suite 305,
3rd Floor, Dilworth Building,
corner Queen and Customs Streets,
Auckland 1
Tel (9) 303 1446   Fax (9) 377 6965

NORWAY
British Tourist Authority,
Nedre Slotts Gt 21,
4 etasje, N-0157 Oslo
Tel (2) 424 745
(as soon as you hear voice, press 200)
Postbox 1554 Vika, N-0117 Oslo

SINGAPORE
British Tourist Authority,
24 Raffles Place,
#19-06 Clifford Centre, Singapore 0104
Tel 535 2966   Fax 534 4703

SOUTH AFRICA
British Tourist Authority,
Lancaster Gate,
Hyde Lane, Hyde Park,
Sandton 2196 *(visitors)*
PO Box 41896, Craighall 2024
(postal address)
Tel (11) 325 0343

SPAIN
British Tourist Authority,
Torre de Madrid 6/5,
Plaza de Espana 18, 28008, Madrid
Tel (1) 541 13 96   Fax (1) 542 81 49

SWEDEN
British Tourist Authority, Klara Norra,
Kyrkogata 29,
S 111 22 Stockholm *(visitors)*
Box 745, S 101 35 Stockholm
(postal address)
Tel (8) 21 24 44   Fax (8) 21 31 29

SWITZERLAND
British Tourist Authority,
Limmatquai 78, CH-8001 Zurich
Tel (1) 261 42 77   Fax (1) 251 44 56

USA
CHICAGO
British Tourist Authority,
625 N Michigan Avenue, Suite 1510,
Chicago IL 60611 *(personal callers only)*

NEW YORK
British Tourist Authority,
551 Fifth Avenue, New York,
NY 10176-0799
Tel 1 800 GO 2 BRITAIN
Fax (212) 986 1188

Three Cliffs Bay, Gower Peninsula

A Brief Guide to the Welsh Language

A few greetings

Welsh	English
Bore da	Good morning
Dydd da	Good day
Prynhawn da	Good afternoon
Noswaith dda	Good evening
Nos da	Good night
Sut mae?	How are you?
Hwyl	Cheers
Diolch	Thanks
Diolch yn fawr iawn	Thanks very much
Croeso	Welcome
Croeso i Gymru	Welcome to Wales
Da	Good
Da iawn	Very good
Iechyd da!	Good health!
Nadolig Llawen!	Merry Christmas!
Blwyddyn Newydd Dda!	Happy New Year!
Dymuniadau gorau	Best wishes
Cyfarchion	Greetings
Penblwydd hapus	Happy birthday

The Welsh National Anthem

Mae hen wlad fy nhadau yn annwyl i mi,
Gwlad beirdd a chantorion enwogion o fri;
Ei gwrol ryfelwyr, gwladgarwyr tra mad,
Dros ryddid collasant eu gwaed.

Chorus

Gwlad! Gwlad! Pleidiol wyf i'm gwlad;
Tra môr yn fur i'r bur hoff bau,
O bydded i'r hen iaith barhau.

The ancient land of my fathers is dear to me,
A land of poets and minstrels, famed men.
Her brave warriors, patriots much blessed,
It was for freedom that they lost their blood.

Chorus

Homeland! I am devoted to my country;
So long as the sea is a wall to this fair beautiful land,
May the ancient language remain.

Pronunciation

There are some sounds in spoken Welsh which are very different from their English equivalents. Here's a basic guide.

Welsh		English equivalent
c	cath *(cat)*	cat (never as in receive)
ch	chwaer *(sister)*	loch
dd	yn dda *(good)*	them
f	y fam *(the mother)*	of
ff	ffenestr *(window)*	off
g	gardd *(garden)*	garden (never as in George)
h	het *(hat)*	hat (never silent as in honest)
th	byth *(ever)*	Three (never as in the)
ll	llaw *(hand)*	

There is no equivalent sound. Place the tongue on the upper roof of the mouth near the upper teeth, ready to pronounce l; then blow rather than voice the l

The vowels in Welsh are a e i o u w y; all except y can be l-o-n-g or short:

long a	tad *(father)*	similar to hard
short a	mam *(mother)*	similar to ham
long e	hen *(old)*	similar to sane
short e	pen *(head)*	similar to ten
long i	mis *(month)*	similar to geese
short i	prin *(scarce)*	similar to tin
long o	môr *(sea)*	similar to more
short o	ffon *(walking stick)*	similar to fond
long w	sŵn *(sound)*	similar to moon
short w	gwn *(gun)*	similar to look

y has two sounds:

1. Clear
dyn *(man)* a long 'ee' sound almost like geese
cyn *(before)* a short 'i' sound almost like tin

2. Obscure
something like the sound in English run, eg:
y *(the)*
yn *(in)*
dynion *(men)*

It is well to remember that in Welsh the accent usually falls on the last syllable but one of a word, eg cadair *(chair)*.

Conwy Castle and town

Get Yourself a Guide

If you want more information or are still undecided on a place to stay, you'll find the answers in this extensive range of publications.

Wales – Bed and Breakfast is one of a series of three official 1996 accommodation guides. All places listed have been checked out by the Wales Tourist Board.

Wales - Hotels, Guest Houses & Farm Houses 1996 £2.95

A wide cross-section of accommodation, with a great choice of places to stay throughout Wales. Something for all tastes and pockets.

Wales - Self-Catering 1996 £2.95

Thousands of self-catering properties, including cottages, flats, chalets and caravan holiday home parks. Also a huge range of parks for touring caravans, motorhomes and tents.

Wales Tourist Map £2

A best-seller – and now better than ever. Detailed 5 miles/inch scale, fully revised and updated. Also includes suggested car tours, town plans, information centres.

A Journey Through Wales £4.80

A magnificent production – 64 big-format pages of the best images in Wales. The 90 photographs take the reader on a tour of Wales's mighty castles, spectacular mountains and coastline, country towns and colourful attractions.

Visitor's Guides to South, Mid and North Wales £3.55 each

Another series of best-sellers, written by Welsh author Roger Thomas. These three information-packed books give you the complete picture of Wales's holiday regions. In full colour – and fully updated.

- Descriptions of resorts, towns and villages
- Where to go and what to see
- Hundreds of attractions and places to visit
- Scenic drives, castles, crafts, what to do on a rainy day
- Detailed maps and town plans

Wales - Castles and Historic Places £7

Describes more than 140 sites in full colour, including castles, abbeys, country houses, prehistoric and Roman remains. A historic introduction sets the scene, and detailed maps help visitors plan their routes.

Wales - A Touring Guide to Crafts £6.80

Specially devised tours in full colour take you to galleries, woodcarvers, potters, jewellers and woollen mills. Nearly 100 craft workshops are listed, together with other places to visit.

'By Car' Guides   £2.30 each

- The Pembrokeshire Coast
- The Brecon Beacons

Two of the 32-page White Horse series. Attractive routes, maps and photographs – the ideal car touring guides to these beautiful parts of Wales.

Ordnance Survey Pathfinder Guides £8.45 each

- Snowdonia Walks (including Anglesey/Llŷn Peninsula)
- Pembrokeshire and Gower Walks
- Brecon Beacons and Glamorgan Walks

80-page books with detailed maps, colour illustrations and descriptions which guide you safely along attractive walking routes.

All prices include postage and packing

FREE PUBLICATIONS

Cycling Wales
See Wales on two wheels. A selection of cycling opportunities, from mountain biking to leisurely routes. Accommodation and cycle hire can be arranged with just one phone call through this brochure.

Discover Wales on Horseback
Full of information on trekking and riding, with a list of accredited centres located throughout Wales, many of which also offer accommodation.

Discovering Accessible Wales
A guide full of ideas and helpful information for people who may have impaired movement or are confined to a wheelchair. Covers everything from accommodation to activities. Available from March 1996.

Freedom Holiday Parks Wales
Caravan Holiday Home Park accommodation in Wales is high on standards and value for money – as you'll see from this brochure which only lists parks graded for quality by the Wales Tourist Board.

Golf in Wales
Beautifully produced large-format guide to Wales's golf courses in full colour, written by Peter Corrigan, Golf Correspondent of the *Independent on Sunday*.

Wales Arts Season '96
Attractive booklet on Wales's thriving and diverse arts scene, with information on events, festivals, theatres, galleries and museums. Available from March 1996.

Wales Touring Caravan and Camping
Detailed guide to Wales Tourist Board-inspected caravan and camping parks which welcome touring caravans, motorhomes and tents.

Walking Wales
A booklet on Britain's most popular leisure activity – and the best place in which to enjoy it. Suggested walks, lists of walking holiday operators and information on the countryside.

The Walled Towns of Wales and Chester
Fascinating 60-page colour guide to medieval walled towns, including Caernarfon, Conwy, Pembroke and Tenby. Historical sites plus tourist information.

PLEASE COMPLETE AND SEND TO: WALES TOURIST BOARD, DEPT BBG96, DAVIS STREET, CARDIFF CF1 2FU

SALEABLE PUBLICATIONS

Please enclose the appropriate remittance in the form of a cheque (payable to Wales Tourist Board) or postal/money order in £ sterling. All prices include post and packing.

☐ Wales – Hotels, Guest Houses & Farm Houses 1996	£2.95	
☐ Wales – Self-Catering 1996	£2.95	
☐ Wales Tourist Map	£2	
☐ A Journey Through Wales	£4.80	
☐ A Visitor's Guide to South Wales	£3.55	
☐ A Visitor's Guide to Mid Wales	£3.55	
☐ A Visitor's Guide to North Wales	£3.55	
☐ Wales – Castles & Historic Places	£7	
☐ Wales – A Touring Guide to Crafts	£6.80	

OS Pathfinder Guides:

☐ Snowdonia Walks *(including Anglesey/Llŷn Peninsula)*	£8.45
☐ Pembrokeshire & Gower Walks	£8.45
☐ Brecon Beacons & Glamorgan Walks	£8.45

'By Car' Guides:

☐ The Pembrokeshire Coast	£2.30
☐ The Brecon Beacons	£2.30

FREE PUBLICATIONS

- ☐ Cycling Wales
- ☐ Discover Wales on Horseback
- ☐ Discovering Accessible Wales
- ☐ Freedom Holiday Parks Wales
- ☐ Golf in Wales
- ☐ Wales Arts Season '96
- ☐ Wales Touring Caravan & Camping
- ☐ Walking Wales
- ☐ The Walled Towns of Wales & Chester

Name *(please print)*: ....

Address *(please print)*: ....

....Post Code: ....

Total remittance enclosed *(if applicable)*: £ ....   Cheque *(payable to Wales Tourist Board)* /PO or Money Order No *(if applicable)*:...........................

Maps of Wales

The maps which follow divide Wales into 12 sections, each with a slight overlap. The grid overlaying each map will help you find the resort, town or village of your choice. Please refer to the map and grid reference which appears alongside the name of each place listed in the 'Where to Stay' gazetteers.

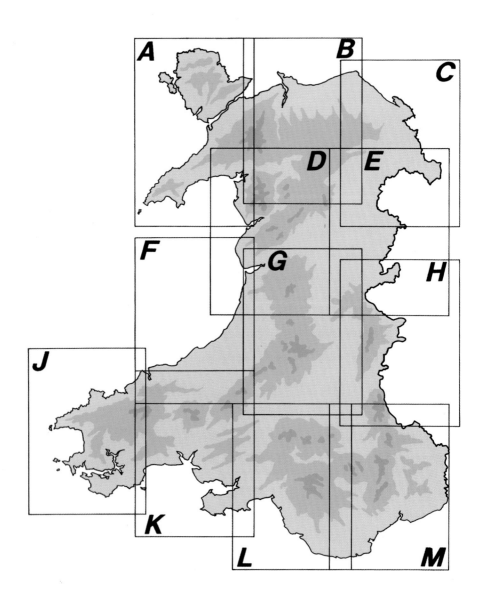

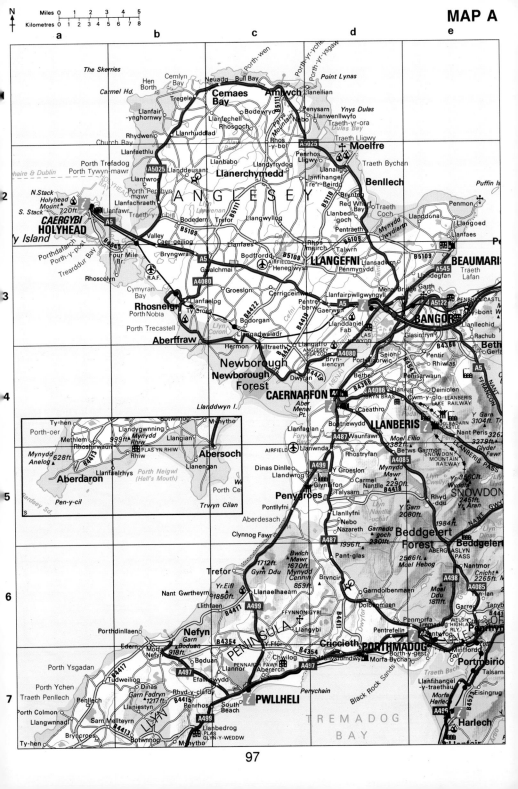

MAP A

97

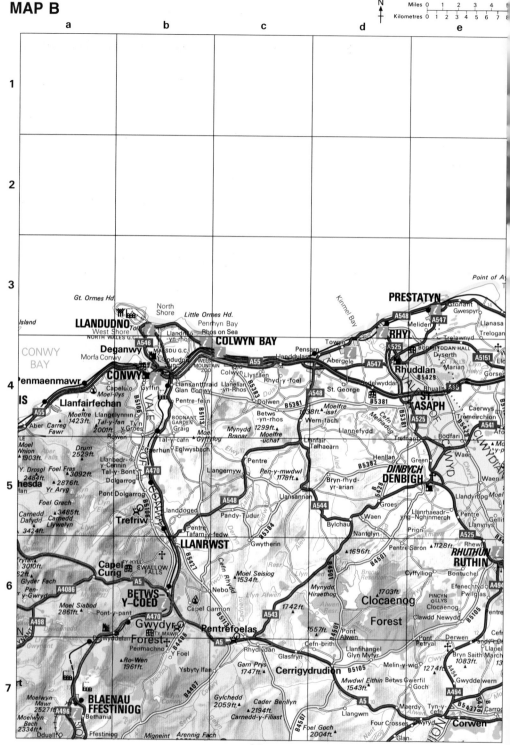

MAP B

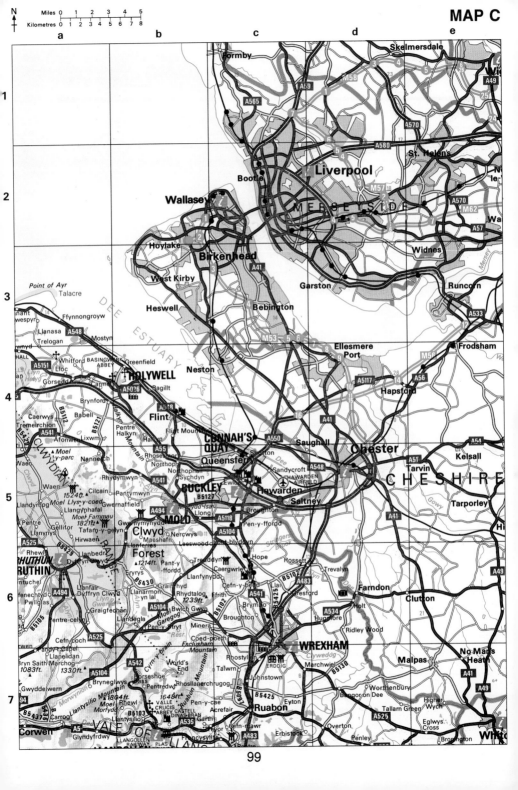

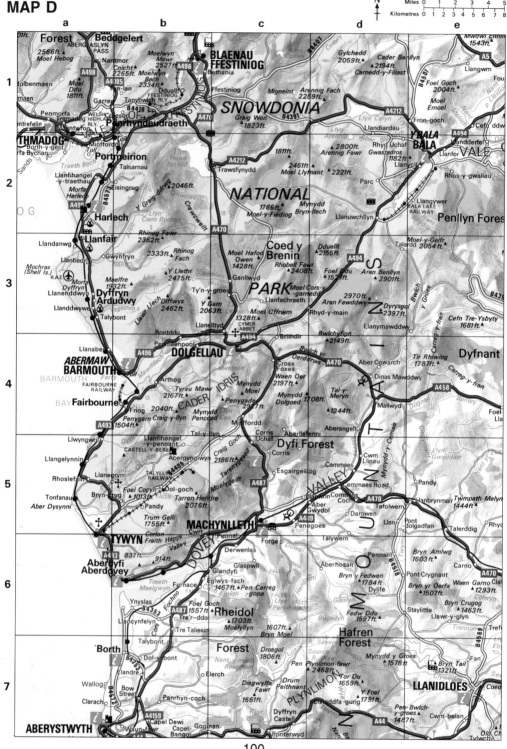

MAP D

N

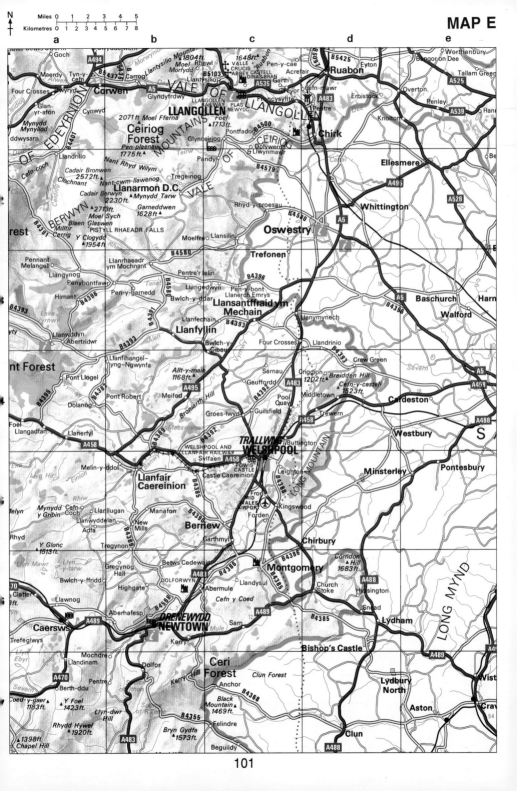

N

Miles 0 1 2 3 4 5
Kilometres 0 1 2 3 4 5 6 7 8

a   b   c   d   e

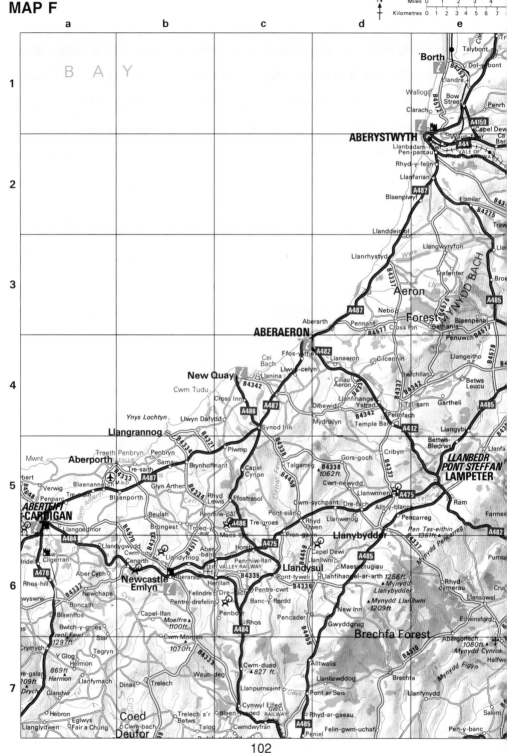

MAP F

a   b   c   d   e

B A Y

Borth   Talybont   Tr
Dol-y-bont
Llandre
Wallog   Bow   Penrh
Street
Clarach   Capel Dew
Ca
Bar
ABERYSTWYTH   Waun-fawr
Llanbadarn-fawr
Pen-parcau   VALE OF
Rhyd-y-felin
Llanfarian
Blaenplwyf   Llanilar
Llanddeiniol

Llangwyryfon
Llanrhystyd   Trefenter   Bro
Aeron   Llyn
Eiddwer
Nebo   Forest   Blaenpenal
Aberarth   Pennant   Bethania   Penuwch
ABERAERON   Cross Inn
Cei   Ffos-y-ffin   Llanaeron   Cilcennin   Llangeitho
Bach   Llwyn-celyn   Bwlchllan
New Quay   Llanina   Ciliau   Betws
Cwm Tudu   Aeron   Leucu
Cross Inn   Llanfihangel   Gartheli
Ynys Lochtyn   Llwyn Dafydd   Dihewid   Ystrad   Tal-sarn
Synod Inn   Mydroilyn   Temple Bar   Llangybi
Llangrannog   Felinfach
Bettws-
Plwmp   Cribyn   Bledrws   Llanfa
Mwnt   Traeth Penbryn Penbryn   Gors-goch   **LLANBEDR**
Aberporth   Samau   Talgarreg   **PONT STEFFAN**
Tre-saith   Brynhoffnant   Capel   B4338   **LAMPETER**
Penparc   Cynon   1062ft.   Cwrt-newydd
Verwig   Blaenannerch   Glyn Arthen   Llanwnnen   Ram
Tremain   Rhyd   Pont-siân   Dre-fach   Allt-y-blaca
Blaenporth   Lewis   Ffostrasol   Pencarreg   Farmer
Beulah   Cwm-sychpant   Pen Tas-eithin
ABERTEIFI   Renmiw-pal   Rhyd   Llanwenog   1361ft.
CARDIGAN   Brongest   Tre-groes   Owen   **Llanybydder**
Llangoedmor   Troed-y-rhiw   Maes   Pron-gwin
Llandygwydd   Aber-   Horeb   New Inn
Cilgerran   Cwm-cou   banc   Llanllwni   Rhyd-
Cenarth   Llandyfriog   Penrhiw-llan   **Llandysul**   cymerau
Rhos-hill   Aber Cych   Aberarad   Pont-tyweli   Llanfihangel-ar-arth   Mynydd   Llansawel
Newchapel   **Newcastle**   Henllan   Pentre-cwrt   Llanybydder
wyswrw   Boncath   **Emlyn**   Felindre Dre-fach   Banc-y-ffordd   Mynydd Llanllwni   Edwinsford
Blaenffos   Pentre-drefelin   1209ft.
Bwlch-y-groes   Capel-Ifan   Penboyr   Pencader   Gwyddgrug   Abergorlech
Trefni Fawr   Moelfre   Mynydd Cynros
1297ft.   1100ft.   **Brechfa Forest**   1080ft.
Crymych   Cwm Morgan   Mynydd Figyn
Y Glog   1070ft.   Alltwalis   Halfw
re-galan   869ft.   Hermon   Tegryn   Cwm-duad
209ft.   Hermon   Llanfyrnach   827 ft.   Brechfa
Drych   Glandwr   Dinas   Trelech   Waun-deg   Llanllawddog   Llanfynydd
Hebron   Eglwys   **Coed**   Trelech a'r   Llanpumsaint   Pont ar Sais   Salem
Fair a Churig   Betws   Taloq   Rhyd-ar-gaeau   Pen-y-banc
Llanglydwen   Cwm-bach   Blaen coed   Cwmdwyfran   Felin-gwm-uchaf
Deufor   Peniel